Praise for MY BROTHER

"Kincaid's haunting memoir of her brother's death from AIDS recounts his troubled life as a Rastafarian involved in the drug culture. Through the larger story of her family's life on Antigua, with emphasis on her mother's powerful personality, Kincaid again illuminates the complex nature of family and intimacy." —*San Francisco Chronicle* Best Books of the Year

"*My Brother* approaches perfection in its controlled prose and detached elegance, with new layers of detail revealed with each recounting of a memory." —GISELLE ANATOL, *Philadelphia Inquirer*

"Kincaid blends the medical with the magical in this riveting memoir of her younger brother Devon, who died of AIDS at age 33. Kincaid's own, accented narration palpably evokes the atmosphere of the island of Antigua, which was her birthplace and the scene of her brother's grueling and strangely instructive death." —CAROLYN ALESSIO, *Chicago Tribune*

"Sober and direct, Ms. Kincaid is unsparing whether looking at others or herself . . . Her unflinching account is all the more poignant for its utter lack of false emotion." —MERLE RUBIN, *The Wall Street Journal*

"Brilliant writing and thinking . . . *My Brother* . . . is about life and death. It's about how economic and emotional poverty corrode the body and the soul. It's about the sticky tentacles that tie brothers to sisters, mothers to daughters, adults to their childhoods, people to where they come from—no matter how far they stray, no matter how desperately they try to escape."
—MEREDITH MARAN, *San Francisco Chronicle Book Review*

"To read Jamaica Kincaid's memoir, *My Brother*, is to re-experience her unforgettable narrative voice, revisiting Antigua over the three years that Devon is dying of AIDS, and re-characterizing the island, her mother and the child/adolescent self chronicled in her earlier books . . . *My Brother* is a memoir of a voice." —GAY WACHMAN, *The Nation*

"Kincaid's prose is, as always, meticulous—the emotions scalding, the declarations harsh. But she triumphs here by transforming tortured memory into emancipating elegy." —NICK CHARLES, *People*

"A poetic, unapologetic chronicle." —*Marie Claire*

"If it is impossible to go home again, it is equally impossible for most of us to stay away . . . Kincaid renders that ambivalence (the tension between revulsion and attachment) so precisely, she makes it seem almost bearable."

—JOAN SMITH, *San Francisco Examiner*

"A narrative of raw, unmediated emotion, this story settles over the reader like a storm. After *My Brother*, everything looks different."

—JULIE HALE, *The Virginian-Pilot*

"Kincaid's prose is so direct, so honest, so searing, so searching that these concise 198 pages demand to be read in one breathtaking sitting."

—JOCELYN MCCLURG, *The Burlington Free Press*

"More than a memoir, *My Brother* is the story of a journey . . . This is another chapter in Kincaid's quest to come to terms with the way politics and history, those two generalities, shape human assumptions in the most specific and idiosyncratic manner." —BETSY WILLEFORD, *The Kansas City Star*

"Kincaid has pulled out all the stops . . . A book whose painful memories meander, then jar the senses like a rattlesnake's tail."

—PAULA L. WOODS, *The Atlanta Journal-Constitution*

"A study in detachment, in bitterness, in survival . . . The memoir crisscrosses time and space from Kincaid's childhood on Antigua to her present-day life in Vermont—as mother, wife, writer—and back again to the hospital ward where her brother lies awaiting a lonely death."

—ELIZABETH MANUS, *The Boston Phoenix Literary Supplement*

Also by Jamaica Kincaid

At the Bottom of the River

Annie John

A Small Place

Lucy

The Autobiography of My Mother

MY BROTHER

JAMAICA KINCAID

Farrar, Straus and Giroux

New York

Farrar, Straus and Giroux
18 West 18th Street, New York 10011

Printed in the United States of America
Published in 1997 by Farrar, Straus and Giroux
First paperback edition, 1998

The Library of Congress has cataloged the hardcover edition as follows:
Kincaid, Jamaica.
My brother / Jamaica Kincaid.
p. cm.
ISBN-13: 978-0-374-21681-8
ISBN-10: 0-374-21681-9 (cloth : alk. paper)
1. Kincaid, Jamaica—Family. 2. Novelists, Antiguan—Family relationships. 3. Women—Antigua—Family relationships. 4. Brothers and sisters—Antigua. 5. Rastafari movement—Antigua. 6. Family—Antigua. I. Title.

PR9275.A583 K5639 1997
813—dc21
[B] *97-16190*

Paperback ISBN-13: 978-0-374-52562-0
Paperback ISBN-10: 0-374-52562-5

Designed by Cynthia Krupat

www.fsgbooks.com

24 26 28 30 29 27 25 23

For Ian ("Sandy") Frazier

WHEN I SAW MY BROTHER again after a long while, he was lying in a bed in the Holberton Hospital, in the Gweneth O'Reilly ward, and he was said to be dying of AIDS. He was not born in this hospital. Of my mother's four children, he was the one born at home. I remember him being born. I was thirteen years of age then. We had just finished eating our supper, a supper of boiled fish and bread and butter, and my mother sent me to fetch the midwife, a woman named Nurse Stevens, who lived on the corner of Nevis and Church Streets. She was a large woman; the two halves of her bottom rolled up and down with each step she took, and she walked very slowly. When I went to give her the message that my mother wanted her to come and assist with my brother's birth, she was just finishing her own supper and said that she would come when she was through. My brother was born in the middle of the night on the fifth of May in 1962. The color of his skin when he was born was a reddish-yellow. I do not know how much he weighed, for he was not weighed at the time he was born. That night, of course, the routine of our life was upset: the routine of my two other brothers and I going to sleep, our father taking a walk to a bridge near the recreation grounds—a walk recommended by his doctor as good for his bad digestive tract and for his bad heart—the heavy black of the streetlampless night falling, our father returning from his walk, a dog barking at the sound of his steps, the door opening and being locked behind him, the click of his false teeth as they were placed in a glass of water, his snoring, and then the arrival of early morning. We were sent to neighbors' houses. I do not remember exactly to whose house my other brothers were sent. I went to the house of a friend of my mother's, a woman whose six-year-old daughter took sick not so very long after this night of my brother's birth and died in my mother's arms on the way to the doctor, exhaling her last breath as they crossed the same bridge that my father walked to on his nightly outing. This was the first person to die in my mother's arms; not long after that, a woman who lived across the street from us, Miss Charlotte was her name, died in my mother's arms as my mother tried to give her some comfort from the pain of a heart attack she was having.

I heard my brother cry his first cry and then there was some discussion of what to do with his after-birth, but I don't know now what was decided to do with all of it; only that a small piece of it was dried and pinned to the inside of his clothes as a talisman to protect him from evil spirits. He was placed in a chemise my mother had made, but because she had two other small children, my other brothers, one of them almost four years old, the other almost two years old, she could not give his chemise the customary elaborate attention involving embroidery stitching and special washings of the cotton fabric; the chemises he wore were plain. He was wrapped in a blanket and placed close to her, and they both fell asleep. That very next day, while they were both asleep, he snuggled in the warmth of his mother's body, an army of red ants came in through the window and attacked him. My mother heard her child crying, and when she awoke, she found him covered with red ants. If he had been alone, it is believed they would have killed him. This was an incident no one ever told my brother, an incident that everyone else in my family has forgotten, except me. One day during his illness, when my mother and I were standing over him, looking at him—he was asleep and so didn't know we were doing so—I reminded my mother of the ants almost devouring him and she looked at me, her eyes narrowing in suspicion, and she said, "What a memory you have!"—perhaps the thing she most dislikes about me. But I was only wondering if it had any meaning that some small red things had almost killed him from the outside shortly after he was born and that now some small things were killing him from the inside; I don't believe it has any meaning, this is only something a mind like mine would think about.

That Thursday night when I heard about my brother through the telephone, from a friend of my mother's because at that moment my mother and I were in a period of not speaking to each other (and this not speaking to each other has a life of its own, it is like a strange organism, the rules by which it survives no one can yet decipher; my mother and I never know when we will stop speaking to each other and we never know when we will begin again), I was in my house in Vermont, absorbed with the well-being of my children, absorbed with the well-being of my husband, absorbed with the well-being of myself. When I spoke to this friend of my mother's, she said that there was something wrong with my brother and that I should call my mother to find out what it was. I said, What is wrong? She said, Call your mother. I asked her, using those exact words, three times, and three times she replied the same way. And then I said, He has AIDS, and she said, Yes.

If she had said he had been in a terrible car accident, or if she had said he was suddenly stricken with a fatal cancer, I would have been surprised, for he did not drive a car—I knew that. What causes a fatal cancer? I do not know that. But he lived a life that is said to be typical in contracting the virus that causes AIDS: he used drugs (I was only sure of marijuana and cocaine) and he had many sexual partners (I only knew of women). He was careless; I cannot imagine him taking the time to buy or use a condom. This is a quick judgment, because I don't know my brothers very well, but I am pretty sure that a condom would not be something he would have troubled himself to use. Once, a few years ago when I was visiting my family—that is, the family I grew up in—I sat on his bed in the house he lived in alone, a house which was two arm's lengths away from our mother's house, where she lived with another son, a grown man, I told him to use condoms when having sex with anyone; I told him to protect himself from the HIV virus and he laughed at me and said that he would never get such a stupid thing ("Me no get dat chupidness, man"). But I might have seemed like a ridiculous person to him. I had lived away from my home for so long that I no longer understood readily the kind of English he spoke and always had to have him repeat himself to me; and I no longer spoke the kind of English he spoke, and when I said anything to him, he would look at me and sometimes just laugh at me outright. You talk funny, he said. And then again, I was not fat, he had expected after not seeing me for twenty years that I would be fat. Most women where we are from become fat after a while; it is fashionable to be a fat woman.

When I saw my brother lying in the hospital bed,

dying of this disease, his eyes were closed, he was asleep (or in a state of something like sleep, because sleep, a perfectly healthy and normal state to be in, could not be what he was experiencing as he lay there dying); his hands were resting on his chest, one on top of the other, just under his chin in that pious pose of the dead, but he was not dead then. His skin was a deep black color, I noticed that, and I thought perhaps I noticed that because I live in a place where no one is of his complexion, except for me, and I am not really of his complexion, I am only of his complexion in the way of race. But many days later my mother said to me, He has gotten so black, the disease has made him so black (she said this to me in this kind of English, she makes an effort to speak to me in the kind of English that I now immediately understand). His lips were scarlet and covered with small sores that had a golden crust. When he opened his eyes and saw me, he made the *truups* sound (this is done by placing the teeth together while pushing out both lips and sucking in air with force all at once). He said he did not think I would come to see him ("Me hear you a come but me no tink you a come fo' true").

At the time the phone call came telling me of my brother's illness, among the many comforts, luxuries, that I enjoyed was reading a book, *The Education of a Gardener*, written by a man named Russell Page. I was in the process of deciding that as a gardener who designed gardens for other people he had the personality of the servant, not the personality of the artist, that his prose was fussy, tidy, timid; though the book bored me I would continue to read it because it offered such an interesting contrast to some other gardeners whose writing I loved. (I only thought all that before the phone rang. I now love *The Education of a Gardener* and look forward to reading it again.) And so when the phone rang I put this book down and answered it and I was told about my brother.

The next time I opened this book I was sitting on the lawn in front of the Gweneth O'Reilly ward and my brother was sitting in a chair next to me. It was many days later. He could barely walk, he could barely sit up, he was like an old man. The walk from his bed to the lawn had exhausted him. We looked out on an ordinary Antiguan landscape. There was a deliberate planting of willow trees, planted, I suspect, a long time ago, when Antigua was still a colony and the colonial government would have been responsible for the running of the hospital. It was never a great hospital, but it is a terrible hospital now, and only people who cannot afford anything else make use of it. Near the willow trees was an old half-dead flamboyant tree; it needed pruning and food. There was an old lop-sided building in the near distance; and the rest of the landscape was taken up with cassi (cassia) trees. And when I picked up that book again, *The Education of a Gardener*, I looked at my brother, for he was a gardener also, and I wondered, if his life had taken a certain turn, if he had caused his life to take a different turn, might he have written a book with such a title? Behind the small house in which he lived in our mother's yard, he had planted a banana plant, a lemon tree, various vegetables, various non-flowering shrubs. When I first saw his little garden in the back of his little house, I was amazed at it and I asked him if he had done it all himself and he said, Of course ("How you mean, man!"). I know now that it is from our mother that we, he and I, get this love of plants. Even at that moment when he and I were sitting on the lawn, our mother had growing on a trellis she had fashioned out of an old iron bedstead and old pieces of corrugated galvanize a passion-fruit vine, and its voluptuous growth was impressive, because it isn't easy to grow passion fruit in Antigua. It produced fruit in such abundance that she had to give some of it away, there was more than she could use. Her way with plants is something I am very familiar with; when I was a child, in the very place where my brother's house is now, she grew all sorts of vegetables and herbs. The red ants that attacked him when he was less than a day old had crawled up some okra trees that she had planted too near the house and the red ants went from the okra trees through a window onto the bed in which he and my mother lay. After she killed all the red ants that had attacked her child, she went outside and in a great fit of anger tore up the okra trees, roots and all, and threw them away.

I only now understand why it is that people lie about their past, why they say they are one thing other than the thing they really are, why they invent a self that bears no resemblance to who they really are, why anyone would want to feel as if he or she belongs to nothing, comes from no one, just fell out of the sky, whole.

For one day when my mother and I were outside in the back yard and she was complaining, though she did not know it, of how dependent on her one or the other of her children was, and did not notice that she did this all the time, said bad things to each of us about the others behind their back, I noticed that the lemon tree my sick brother had planted was no longer there and I asked about it, and she said quite casually, Oh, we cut it down to make room for the addition. And this made me look at my feet immediately, involuntarily; it pained me to hear her say this, it pained me the way she said it, I felt ashamed. That lemon tree would have been one of the things left of his life. Nothing came from him; not work, not children, not love for someone else. He once had a job doing something in the public works department, but he talked back too much—he had a nasty tongue when crossed, my mother said—and one day in an argument with his supervisor he said something rude ("He cuss dem out") and was fired. Someone told me he had made a lot of money then. He gave my mother a lot of it to save for him, but after he was out of work he would often ask her for some of it, until eventually there was nothing left, and when he became sick he was destitute, without any financial support at all. This did not seem to worry him; I could not tell if it had any meaning. When his father, my mother's husband, died, he left my mother a pauper and she had to borrow money to bury him. My brother did not have a steady girlfriend, a woman, someone other than his own mother, to take care of him; he had no children, as he lay dying, his friends had abandoned him. No one, other than the people in his family and his mother's friends from her church, came to visit him.

But this too is a true picture of my mother: When he was ill, each morning she would get up very early and make for her sick son a bowl of porridge and a drink of a fortified liquid food supplement and pack them in a little bag and go to the hospital, which is about a mile away and involves climbing up a rather steep hill. When she set out at about half past six, the sun was not yet in the middle of the sky so it was not very hot. Sometimes someone would give her a lift in a car, but most often no one did. When she got to the hospital, she would give my brother a bath, and when she was doing that she wouldn't let him know that she saw that the sore on his penis was still there and that she was worried about it. She first saw this sore by accident when he was in the hospital the first time, and when she asked him how he got such a thing, he said that from sitting on a toilet seat he had picked up something. She did not believe or disbelieve him when he told her that. After she bathed him, she dressed him in the clean pajamas she brought for him, and if his sheets had not been changed, she changed them and then while he sat in bed, she helped him to eat his food, the food she had prepared and brought to him.

When I first saw him, his entire mouth and tongue, all the way to the back of the inside of his mouth, down his gullet, was paved with a white coat of thrush. He had a small sore near his tonsil, I could see it when he opened his mouth wide, something he did with great effort. This made it difficult for him to swallow anything, but especially solid food. When he ate the porridge and drank the fortified liquid food supplement that my mother had brought for him, he had to make such an effort, it was as if he were lifting tons upon tons of cargo.

A look of agony would come into his eyes. He would eat and drink slowly. Our mother, who loves to cook and see people eat the food she has cooked, especially since she knows she is an extremely good cook, would urge him to eat whenever she saw him pause ("Come on, man, yam up you food") and he would look at her helplessly. Ordinarily he would have made his own sharp reply, but at those moments I do not think one crossed his mind. After she saw him eat his breakfast, she would tidy up his room, put his dirty clothes and bath towel in a bag to be taken home and washed; she would empty the pan that contained his urine, she would rub cream into the parched skin on his arms and legs, she would comb his hair as best she could. My mother loves her children, I want to say, in her way! And that is very true, she loves us in her way. It is *her way*. It never has occurred to her that her way of loving us might not be the best thing for us. It has never occurred to her that her way of loving us might have served her better than it served us. And why should it? Perhaps all love is self-serving. I do not know, I do not know. She loves and understands us when we are weak and helpless and need her. My own powerful memories of her revolve around her bathing and feeding me. When I was a very small child and my nose would become clogged up with mucus, the result of a cold, she would place her mouth over my nose and draw the mucus into her own mouth and then spit it out; when I was a very small child and did not like to eat food, complaining that chewing was tiring, she would chew my food in her own mouth and, after it was properly softened, place it in mine. Her love for her children when they are children is spectacular, unequaled I am sure in the history of a mother's love. It is when her children are trying to be grown-up people—adults—that her mechanism for loving them falls apart; it is when they are living in a cold apartment in New York, hungry and penniless because they have decided to be a writer, writing to her, seeking sympathy, a word of encouragement, love, that her mechanism for loving falls apart. Her reply to one of her children who found herself in such a predicament was "It serves you right, you are always trying to do things you know you can't do." Those were her words exactly. All the same, her love, if we are dying, or if we are in jail, is so wonderful, a great fortune, and we are lucky to have it. My brother was dying; he needed her just then.

In his overbearingly charming reminiscence of how he became a gardener, Russell Page writes:

When I was a child there was a market each Friday in the old Palladian butter market near the Stonebow in Lincoln. The farmers' wives would drive in early in the morning, dressed in their best, with baskets of fresh butter, chickens, ducks and bunches of freshly picked mint and sage. I used often to be taken there by my grandfather's housekeeper while she made her purchases, and I remember that always, in the spring, there would be bunches of double mauve primroses and of the heavenly scented *Daphne mezereum*. Later when my passion for gardening developed I wanted these plants but could never find them in our friends' gardens. They seemed to grow only in cottage gardens in hamlets lost among the fields and woods. I gradually came to know the cottagers and their gardens for miles around, for these country folk had a knack with plants. Kitchen windows were full of pots with cascades of *Campanula isophylla*, geraniums, fuchsias and begonias all grown from slips. I would be given cuttings from old-fashioned pinks and roses which were not to be found in any catalogue, and seedlings from plants brought home perhaps by a sailor cousin—here was a whole world of modest flower addicts.

What would my brother say were he to be asked how he became interested in growing things? He saw our mother doing it. What else? This is what my family, the people I grew up with, hate about me. I always say, Do you remember? There are twelve banana plants in the back of his little house now, but years ago, when I first noticed his interest in growing things, there was only one. I asked my mother how there came to be twelve, because I am not familiar with the habits of this plant. She said, "Well . . ." and then something else happened, a dog she had adopted was about to do something she did not like a dog to do, she called to the dog sharply, and when the dog did not respond, she threw some stones at him. We turned our attention to something else. But a banana plant bears one bunch of fruit, and after that, it dies; before it dies it will send up small shoots. Some of my brother's plants had borne fruit and were dying and were sending up new shoots. The plantsman in my brother will never be, and all the other things that he might have been in his life have died; but inside his body a death lives, flowering upon flowering, with a voraciousness that nothing seems able to satisfy and stop.

I am so vulnerable to my family's needs and influence that from time to time I remove myself from them. I do not write to them. I do not pay visits to them. I do not lie, I do not deny, I only remove myself. When I heard that my brother was sick and dying, the usual deliberation I allow myself whenever my family's needs come up—should I let this affect me or not?—vanished. I felt I was falling into a deep hole, but I did not try to stop myself from falling. I felt myself being swallowed up in a large vapor of sadness, but I did not try to escape it. I became afraid that he would die before I saw him again; then I became obsessed with the fear that he would die before I saw him again. It surprised me that I loved him; I could see that was what I was feeling, love for him, and it surprised me because I did not know him at all. I was thirteen years old when he was born. When I left our home at sixteen years of age, he was three years of age. I do not remember having particular feelings of affection or special feelings of dislike for him. Our mother tells me that I liked my middle brother best of the three of them, but that seems an invention on her part. I think of my brothers as my mother's children.

When he was a baby, I used to change his diapers, I would give him a bath. I am sure I fed him his food. At the end of one day, when he was in the hospital and I had been sitting with him for most of the time, watching his body adjust to the AZT, medicine I had brought to him because I had been told that it was not available in Antigua, I said to him that nothing good could ever come of his being so ill, but all the same I wanted to thank him for making me realize that I loved him, and he asked if I meant that ("But fo' true?") and I said yes, I did mean that. And then when I was leaving for the day and I said good night to him and closed the door behind me, my figure passed the louvered window of his room and from his bed, lying on his back, he could see me, and he called out, "I love you." That is something only my husband and my children say to me, and the reply I always make to them is the reply I made to him: "I love you, too."

He was lying in a small room with a very high ceiling, all by himself. In the hospital they place patients suffering from this disease in rooms by themselves. The room had two windows, but they both opened onto hallways so there was proper ventilation. There was a long fluorescent light hanging from the high ceiling. There was no table lamp, but why should there be, I only noticed because I have become used to such a thing, a table lamp; he did not complain about that. There was a broken television set in a corner, and when there were more than two visitors in the room it was useful as something on which to sit. It was a dirty room. The linoleum floor was stained with rust marks; it needed scrubbing; once he spilled the pan that contained his urine and so the floor had to be mopped up and it was done with undiluted Clorox. He had two metal tables and a chair made of metal and plastic. The metal was rusty and the underside of this furniture was thick with dirt. The walls of the room were dirty, the slats of the louvered windows were dirty, the blades of the ceiling fan were dirty, and when it was turned on, sometimes pieces of dust would become dislodged. This was not a good thing for someone who had trouble breathing. He had trouble breathing.

Sometimes when I was sitting with him, in the first few days of my seeing him for the first time after such a long time, seeing him just lying there, dying faster than most people, I wanted to run away, I would scream inside my head, What am I doing here, I want to go home. I missed my children and my husband. I missed the life that I had come to know. When I was sitting with my brother, the life I had come to know was my past, a past that does not make me feel I am falling into a hole, a vapor of sadness swallowing me up. In that dirty room, other people before him had died of that same disease. It is where they put people who are suffering from the virus that causes AIDS. When he was first told that he had tested positive for the virus, he did not tell our mother the truth, he told her he had lung cancer, he told someone else he had bronchial asthma, but he knew and my mother knew and anyone else who was interested would know that only people who tested positive for the AIDS virus were placed in that room in isolation.

I left him that first night and got into a car. I left him lying on his back, his eyes closed, the fluorescent light on. I rode in a hired car and it took me past the Magdalene maternity ward, where I was born, past the place where the Dead House used to be (a small cottage-like structure where the bodies of the dead were stored until their families came to claim them), but it is not there anymore; it was torn down when it grew rotten and could no longer contain the smells of the dead. And then I came to a major crossing where there was a stoplight, but it was broken and had been broken for a long time; it could not be fixed because the parts for it are no longer made anywhere in the world—and that did not surprise me, because Antigua is a place like that: parts for everything are no longer being made anywhere in the world; in Antigua itself nothing is made. I passed the prison, and right next to it the school my brother attended when he was a small boy and where he took an exam to go to the Princess Margaret School, and in the exam, which was an islandwide exam, he took third place of all the children taking this exam. I passed the Princess Margaret School. It was when he got to this school that he started to get into trouble. My mother says, about the friends he made there, that he fell into bad company, and I am sure the mothers of the other boys, his friends, thought of him in the same way—as bad company. It was while attending this school that he became involved in a crime, something to do with robbing a gas station, in which someone was killed. It was agreed that he did not pull the trigger; it is not clear that he did not witness the actual murder. At some point, years ago, my mother told me that he had spent a short time in jail for this crime and she got him out through political connections she then had but does not have any longer. Now she will not mention the murder or his time in jail. If I should bring it up, she says it is an old story ("e' a' ole time 'tory; you lub ole-time 'tory, me a warn you"), and for my mother an old story is a bad story, a story with an ending she does not like.

The car then turned onto Fort Road and passed Straffee's funeral establishment. I did not know then whether Mr. Straffee was dead or alive; when I was a small child and saw him, I thought he looked like the dead, even though at the time I thought that, I had never seen a dead person. I passed a house where my godmother used to live; she was a seamstress, she had been very nice to me. I do not know what has become of her. And I passed the road where an Englishman, Mr. Moore, who used to sell my mother beefsteak tomatoes, lived. This man also had cows, and one day when I was going to visit my godmother, they were returning from pasture and I saw them coming toward me, and I was so afraid of those cows that I threw myself into a ditch facedown and waited until I knew they had gone by. The road has been widened and the ditch is no more. I passed the place where the Happy Acres Hotel used to be. It, too, is no more. On a road that led from this hotel a friend of our family used to live, a friend whom my brothers would not have known because by the time they were born my mother no longer spoke to this person. The friend reared pigs and guinea hens and chickens and also cultivated an acre or so of cotton. At the height of their friendship my mother had bought shares in a sow this friend of hers owned, and also, since it was at the height of their friendship, I was sent one year to spend August holidays with her. This part of Antigua was considered the country then, and I was terrified of the darkness, it was so unrelieved by light even from other houses; also from the house where I lived I could see the St. John's city graveyard, and it seemed to me that almost every day I could see people attending a funeral. It was then I decided that only people in Antigua died, that people living in other places did not die and as soon as I could, I would move somewhere else, to those places where the people living there did not die. After another minute or so of driving, the car arrived at the inn where I was staying and I went into my room alone, my own isolation.

My mother and I almost quarreled over this, that I would not stay in her house with her. She told a friend of hers, a woman my age, this, knowing that her friend would repeat it to me. I could have said to my mother, You and I do not get along, I am too well, I am not a sick child, you cannot be a mother to a well child, you are a great person but you are a very bad mother to a child who is not dying or in jail; but I did not say that. A few years ago, when she was visiting me in Vermont, we had an enormous quarrel and I then asked her if she could at all say that she was sorry for some of the pain I believe she caused me, whether she meant to or not. And she said then, I am never wrong, I have nothing to apologize for, everything I did at the time, I did for a good reason. Even now, years later, I am still surprised by this, because I spend a good part of my day on my knees in apology to my own children. That time when my mother was visiting me and we had the enormous quarrel, she told a friend of mine, a woman who she knew was very devoted to me, that the reason I did not like her was that when I was a girl she had been very strict with me and if she had not been I would have ended up with ten children by ten different men. It is a mystery to me still why my mother would think I would not be grateful to someone who saved me from such a fate. As an illustration of how strict she had been with me, she told my friend that I loved books and loved reading and there was a boy who used to come around looking for me, and to hide his true intentions, when he saw her he would say that he had come to me to borrow some books; she grew sick of listening to this excuse for his coming around to see me and one day she told him not to come to her house anymore because it was not a library. My friend only told me all this because she wanted to say to me that my mother feels that she loves me very much. But after my mother left, I was sick for three months. I had something near to a nervous breakdown, I suffered from anxiety and had to take medicine to treat it; I got the chicken pox, which is a disease of childhood and a disease I had already had when I was a child. Not long after she left, I had to see a psychiatrist.

My brother who was lying in the hospital dying, suffering from the virus that causes AIDS, told the brother who is two years older than he is, the brother I am eleven years older than, that he had made worthlessness of his life ("Me mek wutless-ness ah me life, man"). He told my mother that he was sorry he had not listened to her when all the time she told him not to behave in the way he had been, not to conduct his life so heedlessly, not to live so much without caution, that he had been too careless. He was sorry now that he lay dying that he had not listened to her and used to think all the things she said she had said only because she was an old lady. He said to me that he couldn't believe he had AIDS ("Me carn belieb me had dis chupid-ness"). Only he could not say the words AIDS or HIV, he referred to his illness as stupidness ("de chupidness").

After I saw my brother that first time and returned to the place I was staying, the place that was not my mother's house, I went to the manageress and said, "I need a drink." I have heard people say just that before, "I need a drink," but I thought it was a figure of speech, I had never needed a drink or any other kind of mood alterer before; I have taken mood-altering substances many times, but I never felt I needed them. I drank five rum-and-Cokes. I do not like the taste of rum, really, and I do not like the taste of Coke, really, but I drank five of these drinks all the same and could have drunk more than five but did not. The manageress, a very nice woman, sat next to me and we struck up a conversation; I told her my brother was sick and in the hospital, and when she asked me the cause of his illness I told her he had AIDS. This disease, in Antigua, produces all the prejudices in people that it produces elsewhere, and so like many other places, the people afflicted with it and their families are ashamed to make their suffering known. It was for my own peace of mind that I said it; I wanted it to be real to me, that my brother was suffering and dying from AIDS; hearing that he was sick and dying was new to me and so every opportunity I got I would say it out loud: "My brother is sick from and dying of AIDS." But my announcing it to this woman led to something. She told me of a doctor in Antigua who she said was always on the radio or television talking about the danger of AIDS, how it could be contracted and how to avoid contracting it. He was considered the leading authority in Antigua in regard to this disease (though in fact he was the only doctor in Antigua who was publicly involved with this disease). She said his name was Dr. Ramsey. The next day I looked him up in the telephone book and called him.

The reason my brother was dying of AIDS at the time I saw him is that in Antigua if you are diagnosed with the HIV virus you are considered to be dying; the drugs used for slowing the progress of the virus are not available there; public concern, obsession with the treatment and care of members of the AIDS-suffering community by groups in the larger non-AIDS-suffering community, does not exist. There are only the people suffering from AIDS, and then the people who are not suffering from AIDS. It is felt in general, so I am told, that since there is no cure for AIDS it is useless to spend money on a medicine that will only slow the progress of the disease; the afflicted will die no matter what; there are limited resources to be spent on health care and these should be spent where they will do some good, not where it is known that the outcome is death. This was the reason why there was no AZT in the hospital; but even if a doctor had wanted to write a prescription for AZT for a patient, that prescription could not be filled at a chemist's; there was no AZT on the island, it was too expensive to be stocked, most people suffering from the disease could not afford to buy this medicine; most people suffering from the disease are poor or young, not too far away from being children; in a society like the one I am from, being a child is one of the definitions of vulnerability and powerlessness.

When I called Dr. Ramsey I asked him if he would meet me at the hospital and examine my brother and give us, his family, medical advice, as to what we could do, what we could not do, what we could expect and, perhaps, when to expect it. He agreed to meet me and at the time he said he would arrive, he arrived. I only mention this because in Antigua people never arrive when they say they will; they never do what they say they will do. He was something I had long ago thought impossible to find in an Antiguan with authority: he was kind, he was loving toward people who needed him, people who were less powerful than he; he was respectful. He greeted my brother as if they were old friends; he spoke to him of cricket, of calypso, and of a trip he had taken to Trinidad to celebrate the carnival there. He examined my brother with his bare hands, he felt his neck, he listened to his breathing through a stethoscope, he looked in my brother's mouth, at his throat, and he made me look at the large ulcer that was near his tonsils. After he was done, he sat and talked to my brother some more; he spoke to him in broken English; I could not understand what they were saying, they spoke very fast, it was the most animated I had seen my brother since I first saw him lying there dying. He even laughed out loud at something Dr. Ramsey said, something I did not understand.

Afterward Dr. Ramsey told me that since my brother did not yet have diarrhea, one of the symptoms common to AIDS sufferers in the Caribbean, there was a chance that AZT could slow the progress of the disease and allow my brother to live longer than we thought; certainly it would alleviate some of his immediate suffering. When I had heard about my brother, I asked my mother with what medicines he was being treated and she said they were giving him something for pneumonia and something else for thrush, medicines a doctor at the hospital had given her a prescription for and she had gone to a pharmacy in town and purchased. These medicines common in the treatment of AIDS-related illnesses are not kept in the hospital; people who are not infected with the virus that causes AIDS do not get an extreme case of thrush, do not get a terrible kind of pneumonia, and so the medicines that would treat these afflictions are not on hand at the hospital. But then this: one night my brother had a terrible headache and needed something to ease the pain; there was no aspirin on the ward where he was staying and no aspirin in the dispensary. A nurse on duty had some in her purse for her own personal use and she gave my brother two of them. There are people who complain that a hospital in the United States will charge six dollars for a dose of Tylenol; they might wish to look at this way of running a hospital: bring your own medicines.

When my mother told me AZT could not be obtained in Antigua, I called someone I know, a friend who is a doctor, and I asked her if she would write a prescription for a month's worth. She said yes immediately, and said she would give me more if it was necessary. I was used to this sort of kindness. I did not know then if even a month's worth would be of any use to him. She gave me a prescription for a more powerful drug than the one he was taking to treat the pneumonia he had and a more powerful drug than the one he was taking to treat his thrush; when I first saw him, the thrush had made it so difficult for him to swallow anything that the pills had to be crushed before he could swallow them.

After he saw my brother, Dr. Ramsey told me that, with one exception, he had not seen anyone over the age of thirty-two suffering from AIDS. The exception was a man sixty-six years of age. He said that in August one year, in a two-week period, seven people, young people, all under thirty-two, had died of the disease. As far as he could tell, the people who died did not know each other. He said that people who are not HIV-positive give up too soon on the people who are, but that he tries to keep everybody alive, because you never know when a cure might come along. He said that—you never knew when a cure might come along—and I could not tell if, in that, he was asserting native Antiguan foolishness or faith in science. Antigua is a place in which faith undermines the concrete. He said my brother did not look too bad, he had seen people who looked worse; what he meant of course is he had seen people who were on the verge of dying, and by the time he saw them, it was too late to do anything. But what could he do, I wanted to ask him, if there was no medicine available, if the people suffering did not have a sister who lived in the United States and this sister could call up a doctor who would write a prescription for some medication that might be of help, what would happen then? He is a very loving man and the other reason I have for saying this is I saw that wherever he went, people, ordinary people, would go out of their way to greet him and ask him how he was, but not because they really wanted to know: it was just to hear his voice.

I went to hear Dr. Ramsey give a lecture about AIDS and other sexually transmitted diseases to a group of twelve people who were attending a workshop on counseling the HIV-afflicted. I had never seen any of their faces before. Among them were a man and a woman, Antiguans, whose thirty-year-old daughter had died of AIDS. She was their only child. They carried with them pictures of her which they showed to the other people in the workshop. They were attending this workshop because they hoped to be able, if need be, to give solace to other parents who might also find themselves losing a child to this disease. This was something very new to me: ordinary people in Antigua expressing sympathy and love for one another at a time of personal tragedy and pain, not scorn or rejection or some other form of cruelty. Dr. Ramsey explained to us what the HIV virus is, how it behaves in the body, how a virus behaves and how the HIV virus, a retrovirus, differs from a normal virus, but I cannot really remember any of it because he showed extraordinary slides of people in various stages of affliction from sexually transmitted diseases. The pictures were amazing. There were penises that looked like ladyfingers left in the oven too long and with a bite taken out of them that revealed a jam-filled center. There were labias covered with thick blue crusts, or black crusts, or crusts that were iridescent. There were breasts with large parts missing, eaten away, not from a large bite taken at once but nibbled, as if by an animal in a state of high enjoyment, each morsel savored for maximum pleasure. There were pictures of people emaciated by disease, who looked very different from people emaciated from starvation; they did not have that parched look of flesh and blood evaporated, leaving a wreck of skin and bones; they looked like the remains of a black hole, something that had once burned brightly and then collapsed in on itself. These images of suffering and death were the result of sexual activity, and at the end of Dr. Ramsey's talk, I felt I would never have sex again, not even with myself. This feeling I had of pleasure being overwhelmed by fear and death was not new; I remembered how as a child when I was living in Dominica with my mother's family I would look up at a black sky with a big moon full of light in it and the large mountains in the distance silhouetted against the mysterious (to me, a small girl) horizon, and I would find this the most beautiful, the most wonderful thing in the world, but then I would see a light moving about in the mountains and knew that it was a jablessé and would run inside to bed and pull the sheets over my head. And lying in bed with the sheets over my head, I would become afraid to fall asleep with the sheets over my head because I might suffocate and die.

Someone told me that many years ago Dr. Ramsey led an effort to make women in Antigua conscious of methods of birth control and that it was a success, because had I noticed that every woman of child-bearing age was not pregnant anymore? It is true that every woman of child-bearing age is not pregnant, but I had not noticed it; I take it for granted that every woman of child-bearing age does not have a child if she does not want to. Dr. Ramsey told me that when he first started to talk to Antiguans about sexually transmitted diseases, and in particular AIDS, men would say that he was lying, that he was being unnecessarily alarming, and, jokingly, that he had an ulterior motive ("Me no go wid Ramsey, you know, 'e just want to keep all de women fo' 'eself"). He told me that one night he gave a talk to some young people about AIDS and other sexually transmitted diseases. Afterward two young men asked him for a lift, and when they reached a certain part of town, a part of town where prostitutes live, they asked to be let out. Dr. Ramsey asked them if they had condoms and they said no. He asked them if they had not listened to anything he had just told them, and they said to him yes, but they would rather die than leave the butter women alone ("Me rather dead dan leave butta women 'lone"). The prostitutes in Antigua are from Santo Domingo. They are mostly light-brown-skinned black women. Because of their complexion, Antiguan men call them butter women. It is believed that a majority of them are HIV-positive.

I did not know how my brother had contracted the HIV virus. I would have liked to know because it would have told me something about him. I was almost sure it was not through the use of intravenous drugs, because there was no evidence of that on his body as far as I could see; also, such a thing as piercing himself with a needle, causing himself pain, did not seem to be in keeping with his personality; the use of intravenous drugs involves hypodermic needles and hypodermic needles would be associated with illness and death. In a place like Antigua, I suspect, the use of drugs is not about the dulling of pain in a useless life but about providing and extending pleasure. I do not know this with certainty, I only suspect so. I suspected he got the virus through sex and I supposed it to be heterosexual sex. I only supposed this, I did not know it with any certainty. If he had had homosexual sex, he would not have advertised it. Antiguans are not particularly homophobic so much as they are quick to disparage anyone or anything that is different from whom or what they think of as normal. And they think of themselves and the things they do as normal: this includes a man and a woman having sex with each other. I only wanted to know these things about my brother because they would tell me something about him, but also, on the whole I like to know whom people have sex with, and a description of it I find especially interesting. My own life, from a sexual standpoint, can be described as a monument to boring conventionality. And so perhaps because of this I have a great interest in other people's personal lives. I wanted him to tell me what his personal life had been like. He would not do that. Antiguans are at once prudish and licentious. A young woman will be loudly praised for being a very nice girl, by which it is meant she does not have sex; yet no young woman would ever be ostracized because she had ten children by ten different men.

He used to have many friends, they were at his house visiting him all the time before he got sick, when he was well, with no thought of sickness at all. They were young men like him, Rastafarians like him. They would come to his house and sit on his bed and smoke fat marijuana cigarettes. My mother would complain about these young men visiting her son, but her words of complaint did not stop them and she did not go further than words. These boys had Rastafarian names, names they had given themselves, names very different from the ones their parents had given them. My brother's Rastafarian name was the name of a Hebrew prophet, one whose prophecies were about pestilence and doom. But when he lay in the hospital, none of his friends came into his room to visit him. They came to see him. They would stand in the doorway of his room and they would say something to him. They never came in. After they had seen him they left and they never returned again. My mother said that they came to see if it was true that he was HIV-positive, that he had AIDS. Had he been in their shoes, he might have done the same thing. We are not an instinctively empathetic people; a circle of friends who love and support each other is not something I can recall from my childhood. A girl he used to know saw him in the hospital while I was there with him. I could not tell if she had been one of his lovers. He and I were sitting outside in the sun at the time. He spoke in a very friendly way to her; she was friendly but not too much so, she never came too near him. She went inside to visit someone else. When she came outside to leave, she did not come over to say goodbye to him. He called after her. She waved her hand at him without looking back. He asked her if she would come back to see him. She raised her shoulders high, in an I-don't-know gesture. She never looked back at him. But not long after, while we were still sitting in the sun, he saw a woman wearing a pair of tight-fitting pants that outlined the curves around her pubic area, and while staring pointedly at her crotch, he said some words to her, letting her know that he would like to have sex with her ("That would fit me very nicely, you know." He said it exactly like that). She, too, would not look at him. This made me wonder at the confidence of men. There he was, diseased and dying, looking as unattractive as a long-dead corpse would look, and he could still try to convince a woman to sleep with him.

One day years ago—I was thirty-six and he was twenty-three—I was visiting my family, I was lying on my brother's bed in his little house with my feet resting on the windowsill and in the sun. I used to do exactly this when I was a child: lie in bed with my feet resting on the windowsill and in the sun, because my feet then were always cold. I would read books then, and this whole scene of me lying in bed and reading books would drive my mother to fits of anger, for she was sure it meant I was doomed to a life of slothfulness, but as it turned out, I was only doomed to write books other people might read. At the time I was lying on my brother's bed, he was sitting in his doorway. Usually he was lying on his bed. He would lie on his bed in a drug-induced daze. His mother would not have allowed him to do this if he were female; I know this. The walls of his house were plastered with magazine pictures of Americans who have been extremely successful in the world of sports or entertainment. All these people are of my and his complexion. My daughter likes to sing. It is perhaps the pictures on my brother's wall that make me discourage her from singing in a way that might bring her public attention. I have said to her father, "Does the world really need one more somewhat brown person singing?" My daughter loves math and is very good at it. Maybe she can find satisfaction singing to herself while poring over numbers that will explain some small mystery in the universe. There may be someone of my brother's hue, or my daughter's hue, or my own hue who has been awarded the Nobel Prize for physics or chemistry, but if such a person exists, my brother does not know of it, my daughter may know of it, I do not know of it. In his room that time were some books on a table and a radio cassette-deck player. The books were his old school textbooks. One of them was a history of the West Indies, though it was mostly a history of the British West Indies, and it was exactly like the textbook from which I had been taught when I was in school. I was reading it, lying on his bed, and when I got up to go, he gave it to me as a gift. I still have this book, it's sitting on a shelf with some other books that I like very much.

He must have wanted to be a singer. He had a stage name, it was Sugarman. He had on cassette tape a recording of him and a friend of his singing a song called "Mr. Telephone Man." It was a song that was popular not too long ago, sung by a group called "The Silvers"; these people, "The Silvers," were all related to each other, they were not just friends. He and his friend sang this song in the reggae style. He gave me a copy of this tape of him and his friend singing this song. I lost it when moving from one house to another. I am only sorry about this now.

On the morning I was leaving my brother, after spending a week with him, we learned he had gained one pound. It was a Monday morning; I had arrived a week ago on the Sunday night and he had looked then as if he would soon die: he was losing weight, he could not eat, his temperature would go from high to dangerously high, his throat had large ulcers growing on the surface and they went all the way down his esophagus. Everyone thought it was a matter of days, weeks, but all the same he would soon be dead. I had brought him the medicine AZT, he took it and did begin to look better. His temperature had dropped down, not to normal, but to below normal; Dr. Ramsey said that was better than being too high. And then just as I was leaving to return home to my own family on an early-morning flight, he, along with the other patients on his ward (all men suffering from various ailments, none of them related to HIV, as far as I could tell, since they were not treated with the aloofness, at-arm's-lengthness, that was extended to my brother), were lined up in the hall to be weighed on an ancient but accurate-seeming scale. The scale registered a one-pound gain in my brother's weight from the week before. I felt happy, I felt pleased with myself, I even felt proud of myself. I had been instrumental in this, his gaining one pound, and I knew what it meant; it meant that he was getting better, or at least that he was better than he had been before I got there, when every time he had stepped on the scale it had registered a loss. The nurse who recorded this on his chart, a Sister, a rank of nursing that continues to exist only in places where the British influence, with its love of status, remains, turned the corners of her mouth down as she did so. This must be a universal expression of disappointment and irritation and sourness, but I have seen it only in the disappointed and the irritated and the sour among women in Antigua. He had been expected to die; no one infected with HIV and as sick as he was at that time had ever come out of the Holberton Hospital alive. I said goodbye to him, he thought I would not come to see him again. I said I would come again, and it crossed my mind and he said it out loud, yes, perhaps to his funeral ("Yu cum back fo' bury me").

I got on the airplane. As I was going through

Customs in Puerto Rico, I wondered what he was doing. He might be sitting out in the sun, the way he and I had done in the few days when I had been there. He might be able to focus his eyes and concentrate now, he might be able to control the tremor in his hands and so be able to read the biography of Viv Richards, the great Antiguan cricketer, a copy of which I had bought for him. As I was going through Customs I remembered a British woman of African descent whom I had met at a workshop she was leading for people who wanted to volunteer to be AIDS counselors. When she found out that I lived in the United States and that my brother was lying in the hospital more dead than alive and because this was due to a lack of proper treatment, she said, as if it were the most natural, obvious suggestion in the world, that I should take him to the United States for treatment. I was stunned by this, because I was doing the best I could, I have a family, I'm not rich, everybody who comes in contact with this disease knows how costly it is to deal with properly; she in her position as leader of workshops would have known so, how could she just say things without asking about my circumstances, without wondering what taking my brother into my life would mean to me. I said, Oh, I am sure they wouldn't let him in, and I didn't know if what I was saying was true, I was not familiar really with immigration policies and HIV, but what I really meant was, no, I can't do what you are suggesting—take this strange, careless person into the hard-earned order of my life: my life of children and husband, and they love me and love me again, and I love them. And then she said, Oh yes, racism. And I thought then, with more bitterness than I would have otherwise, how unlucky people are who cannot blame the wrong, disastrous turns life can sometimes take on racism; because the hardness of living, the strange turns in it, the luck of it, the good chance missed of it, the there-but-for-the-grace-of-God part of it is so impossible to accept and it must be, in some way, very nice to have the all too real evil of racism to blame. But it was not racism that made my brother lie dying of an incurable disease in a hospital in the country in which he was born; it was the sheer accident of life, it was his own fault, his not caring about himself and his not being able to carefully weigh and adjust to and accept the to-and-fro of life, the feasting and the famine of life or the times in between, it was the fact that he lived in a place in which a government, made up of people with his own complexion, his own race, was corrupt and did not care whether he or other people like him lived or died.

I returned to my home safely, and my family was glad to see me. I called my mother. It was the middle of winter and I missed the warm sun and I missed my brother, being with him, being in the presence of his suffering and the feeling that somewhere in it was the possibility of redemption of some kind, though what form it could take I did not know and did not care, only that redemption of some kind would be possible and that we would all emerge from it better in some way and would love each other more. Love always feels much better than not-love, and that is why everybody always talks about love and that is why everybody always wants to have love: because it feels much better, so much better. I missed him sometimes when I took my children to the school bus, sometimes when the snow fell; I talked about him, his life, to my husband, I talked about him to people I knew well and to people I did not know very well. But I did not think I loved him; then, when I was no longer in his presence, I did not think I loved him. Whatever made me talk about him, whatever made me think of him, was not love, just something else, but not love; love being the thing I felt for my family, the one I have now, but not for him, or the people I am from, not love, but a powerful feeling all the same, only not love. My talk was full of pain, it was full of misery, it was full of anger, there was no peace to it, there was much sorrow, but there was no peace to it. How did I feel? I did not know how I felt. I was a combustion of feelings.

My brother grew better and better; the AZT must have worked, he grew stronger, his clogged lungs cleared up, the sores in his throat began to disappear. One day, still in hospital, he rejected the food served to him and the food my mother brought to him, and asked for a serving of Kentucky Fried Chicken, that was the thing he most wanted to eat then. A franchise of this restaurant is in Antigua and it is a fashionable place to go, to be able to afford to buy and eat a meal purchased there. Dr. Ramsey was visiting him at the time he had this craving, and so he drove my mother to the restaurant, where she bought him a dinner of fried chicken, and she took a taxi back to the hospital and gave it to him.

He ate it all and my mother was very happy because she had not seen him eat so heartily in months. She reported this to me with as much enthusiasm and satisfaction as if she had just seen him successfully complete a feat that no human had ever successfully completed before. In the days to come he grew more and more well, he ate more, his temperature was a little below normal, but it remained the same, it did not go up and it did not go way up. And then everyone began to wonder what to do with him, how long should he be in the hospital, should he still be in the hospital? No one had ever seen an HIV-infected person, who in fact had full-blown AIDS, leave the hospital in this condition—alive, even well; well if you did not know what his life was really, really like. He by then was sitting outside in the company of the other patients; they no longer shunned him, because he did not look like someone who had AIDS, he looked just like an ordinary sick person; an ordinary sick person was something they knew about, a person with AIDS was not. He looked like them, sick with no choice but to go to an ill-equipped hospital in Antigua. While he was in the hospital, another man came in, very sick with AIDS, as sick as my brother had been. The man died. His relatives did not come to see him. I do not know if my brother visited him and offered any words of comfort. My brother by then was well enough to go home. But what home? He did not really have a home. He would go home to live with my mother, and this was wonderful, that he would live with his mother and she would take care of him, but this became another example of the extraordinary ability of her love for her children to turn into a weapon for their destruction.

My mother lives with her male children, who by now are in their thirties, or rather, my mother's male children, by now in their thirties, live with her. It is an important distinction. My mother would not subordinate herself in any way to anyone, especially not her children. She would not live with anyone; they would live with her; if she were to live with anyone, they might ask her to leave, they might throw her out after she had given them one of her famous tongue-lashings. She protects and reserves her right to verbally humiliate her children. What can be so wrong with that? She and the grown-up men children who live with her quarrel all the time. At any given moment there is a small war of words going on between her and one of them. The middle grown-up male child no longer speaks to her; it has been years since he has spoken to her in even so much as the tone of voice he would use for giving directions to someone he just met on the street, someone he has never seen before. If he is forced to speak to her, his voice is full of hatred and despair. He has told me he does not recognize the sound of his own voice when he speaks to her. He calls me up to tell me he is sorry he never sympathized with me when I told him how awful she had been to me. He says to me, Mom is evil, you know, as if he had never said it to me before, but he says it to me every time we speak, as if it is a new discovery to him.

After he was dismissed from the hospital my brother went back to my mother's house and slept in her bed with her. He had no place to go, not even a bed of his own, and so he went to his mother's house and slept in her bed with her. There was nothing wrong with that. It was decided that the son coming home from the hospital should move into her bed because his old house, which was behind hers, was too drafty. I could not understand this, because what kind of draft exists in a place that is hot all the time? There was another reason for him going to live with her. The oldest of her three sons had been living in the other shack behind her house, and his living quarters were really just pieces of galvanize all nailed together with one opening, which was the door. The structure that my sick brother had lived in resembled an actual house; it had three windows and the windows had working shutters, it had a door that could be bolted. When my brother went to the hospital because he was so sick, the one living in the galvanized house immediately moved into the sick boy's place and my mother could not and would not tell him to move back to his old structure. These two brothers did not get along; I was told this, they did not get along, as if it were an exception, as if usually the people in this family got along except for those two. It was my mother who told me that they did not get along, and she gave me an example of their disagreement. The brother living in the room made of old galvanize is an electrician and he has many valuable tools, which he kept in his room; at the height of my sick brother's drug addiction, he would go into his brother's room and remove tools, which he would then sell. My brother the electrician, after warning his brother not to steal from him, ran a live wire around the perimeter of his room and did not tell anyone. A puppy that had been a parting present to my friend who was moving to St. Vincent ran into the live wire and was electrocuted. My mother said she was sure that one brother had not meant to kill the other, that he would not have used wires that carried current strong enough to do so.

This was the home my brother was discharged to. He went home with his mother. He had gained more weight. His temperature was normal. He had an enormous appetite. The infections in the throat, the lungs, the thrush, all of them had cleared up. He only took his daily doses of AZT and a tonic, a high-powered multivitamin, that Dr. Ramsey had prescribed for him. We spoke to each other on the telephone; sometimes he called me, mostly I called him, almost every day. He did not sound like his old self. His voice sounded like that of someone who has just inhaled an amount of helium, out of its normal register. He would speak to me with a pretend English accent, making fun of the way I have come to speak, I suppose, but meaning no malice, I believe, and even if he did, I don't believe I would care; that, after all, is not serious malice.

He would say, How are you, maiy deahre, and how is the home front? In his own voice he would tell me that he felt as if he could take on the world, he felt better than he had ever felt, that life looked wonderful, that he was going to change everything, how sorry he was that he had let things go like that, he had wasted his life, he was going to look for a job as soon as he was able, the doctor had said that just now he should rest and gain some more weight, but as soon as he could get a job, he wanted to settle down and start a family. He would say that again and again, he wanted his own family and as soon as he could, he would get to it. He told me of a plot of land that was bare, available, for sale; he was going to buy it and build a house there and raise a family there. Perhaps it was a flag of some kind, he was trying to tell me something, I don't know; anyway, why should I tell him just now when he sounded so full of promise, so full of happiness, that a family of the kind he wanted, a woman bearing his own children, was not ever going to be possible? I missed him. I missed seeing him suffer. I missed feeling sorry that I could see him in his suffering, I missed seeing him in the midst of something large and hoping he would emerge from it changed for the better. I did not love him. What I felt might have been love, but I still, even now, would not call it so.

His doctor, Dr. Ramsey, called to ask if I thought he was all right, if I knew anything about the life he was leading now, if he was seeing his old friends again; and this was because on one of his visits for a checkup, he had asked one of Dr. Ramsey's nurses to go out on a date with him, and when she mentioned his illness he denied he was infected with the virus that causes AIDS, and then when he knew that Dr. Ramsey knew of his behavior he demanded to be tested again for the HIV virus because he said he did not believe he was in a positive condition. Dr. Ramsey thought from the sound of his voice perhaps he was on drugs again. I told the doctor that I believed the sound of his voice was from being so glad to be alive. I believed that then, I believe it now. I said, He is so glad to be alive, his voice has the sound natural to someone glad to be alive. But how did I know that? It was not from personal experience. It was only from conjecture on my part. If I had been almost dead, expected to be dead and then found I was alive, I believe my voice would be suffused with the sound of happy disbelief. I imagined him sitting on my mother's little front porch, watching the sun's heat lose its grip on land and people, the paper-thin white clouds drift by, going one way, seldom returning thick and black with rain; the unnatural-to-a-small-island sound of car horns signaling a traffic jam, the impatience of people in a hurry to get to destinations that are never much more than a stone's throw away. Whenever anyone passed by, he would have to call out to them a greeting regardless of whether they were familiar to him or not. He would not be able to bear the emptiness of silence, someone passing by with no knowledge of his existence, someone passing by who wants no knowledge of his existence. He was not meant to be silent. He was a brilliant boy, he was a brilliant man. Locked up inside him was someone who would have spoken to the world in an important way. I believe this. Locked up inside him was someone who would have found satisfaction speaking to the world in an important way, and that someone would not have needed to greet every passerby, that someone would not have time for every passerby, that someone would have felt there isn't enough silence in the world. But he was not even remotely aware of such a person inside him. It is I who told him this and he agreed with me at the moment I told him this, and he said yes, and I saw that he wished what I said were really true, would just become true, wished he could, wished he knew how to make the effort and make it true. He could not. In his daydreams he became a famous singer, and women removed their clothes when they heard him sing.

He and my mother both called me to say that he had no more AZT. I panicked because I believed even one day of missing his treatment might cause a setback. If only they had told me that he would be needing more before he needed more. Why hadn't I thought of it? I called the doctor in this country who had given me the prescription in the first place; the doctor called the pharmacy. It was a Friday afternoon, the pharmacy had no more AZT left and would not be getting any more until the following Monday morning. It suddenly dawned on me that there might be quite a few people in my little community who needed this drug. I did not know who they were. If I wanted to know it was only because I now in some way felt related to them. That Monday I got the AZT, I sent it to my brother through a private mail service, he received it, he resumed taking it; a few days without it in his system did not seem to make any difference to his physical well-being. He continued to gain strength, he continued to get well.

It had been six weeks since I had seen my brother, six weeks since the morning I left him in the hospital, shortly after he had been weighed and registered a gain of one pound from the week before. I had returned home to my family, to winter that, as it must, turns to spring. I wanted to go and see him again and I was preparing to do so when in a conversation I was having with my son I mentioned my mother. I said, My mother . . . but before I could get any further, my son said, Your mother, I didn't even know you had a mother. He knew very well I had a mother, he had even met her. The time when she had come to visit me and I had a nervous breakdown after she left, he was two years old. Perhaps he was too young to remember that he did not like her, only for the reason that he did not like anyone for whom I had powerful feelings; he might have felt that any powerful feelings I had for anyone else meant less powerful feelings left for him. The way he said it, though, alerted me to something. He had not known or imagined that I, his own mother, could have in her life a someone about whom I felt the same way he felt about me. When he looks at me he does not see a person, he sees the sky blotted out, the horizon, too; there is no B.C.E. or C.E., there is no present or future, there is no time at all; he sees his needs fulfilled, his needs unfilled, he sees satisfaction and disappointments, I am for him a source of pleasure and pain, he shall wish me dead many times, and when I finally do die, a large emptiness that can never be filled up will be with him for the rest of his own life; he loves me now and hates me now, too, though this last he does not yet fully understand. This state of profound contradiction, loving me and hating me, is what will be for the rest of his life, if I am a good mother to him. This is the best that it can be. If I should fail him—and I very well might, the prime example I have is not a good one—he will experience something everlastingly bitter and awful; I know this, the taste of this awfulness, this bitterness, is in my mouth every day.

Feeling, then, that my son—my children—needed to see me as vulnerable to someone as they are to me, I took them with me on the next visit I made to see my brother, which meant being in the company of my mother. They loved her; my children loved my mother, especially my daughter. My daughter asked her to come and eat with us, to come swimming with us, to come and sleep with us. She wanted to see her grandmother all the time. My son felt the same way, except he complained that he didn't like the way my mother pinched his cheek when she asked him if he was really her little grandson. They ate whatever she cooked for them. I would say to her, They have no appetite, they never eat anything, and she would say they ate everything she had put on their plate. This was true. It amazed me the amount of food they ate when my mother cooked for them. My mother, looking at my children, told me that they loved her ("Dem lub me. Dem lub me a lot, you know"), and there was something strange in this, as if in time they would come to love her more than they loved me, and there was something boastful in it, as if to say that everyone eventually loves her, as if to say that anyone who loves me will love her, only more so. I told her only that this was true, that they did love her; I did not tell her that loving your grandmother a lot was to be expected, that it was something common, like standing in the open anywhere in the world and looking up and seeing the sky. My brother when he saw my children asked if I had brought them to see him before he died ("Yu bring dem fo' see me before me dead"). He said it sharply, he said it directly, he actually looked me in the face. I thought he might laugh, I thought he might cry. I did not answer. I did not say that had not crossed my mind.

My brother looked well, very very well. He said he felt well, very very well. I thought, He may be dying, but he's not dying as rapidly as he was before; I may be dying much more quickly than he; I could cross the street and a car could run over me; he may outlive us all; anything could happen. I wanted then to call some of the people who had been kind to him and helped him when he was sick. I called a man who would come to the house and give my mother a ride to the hospital for her second visit of the day every day. This was extremely kind, the sun would be at its hottest then. I thanked some other people. I called a woman, a social worker, who counseled families in which a member was HIV-positive. When my brother first took sick, someone had told me to get in touch with her. When my brother first met her, he denied to her that he was HIV-positive. It was after many visits with her that he began to say of himself that he was infected with the HIV virus, or that he had AIDS, though he still called it "the chupidness." For him to face honestly and straightforwardly his affliction was thought to be a good thing, because it meant then that he might somehow begin to understand what was happening to him and try to cope with this stage of his life and so live as long as possible. When my brother asked me if I had brought my children to see him before he died, that to me was evidence that the work she had done with him was a success. And so I called and thanked her. I asked her how she thought he was doing. She said he looked well, but she did not like the tonic he took because the main ingredient in it was alcohol, she had asked him not to take it, he did not need it, Dr. Ramsey had given him vitamins in tablet form that were more than adequate; he took this tonic not in the measured, prescribed amount but from the bottle itself. She was annoyed, I could tell. I said I was sorry. She said there was more. She was gloomy now, I could tell. She had come to visit my brother one day, and a girl from Guiana was there ("a Guianese girl": she was expressing prejudice here, life in Antigua is better than life in Guiana; people will come from Guiana to do the work that Antiguan people like my brother will no longer do). After the girl left, she got answers to questions she had not really meant to ask; she had not come prepared to ask these questions, it occurred to her to mention them only because she saw the girl. My brother had been having unprotected sex with this woman and he had not told her that he was infected with the HIV virus. He did not tell her, because if he told her he thought she might not want to have sex with him at all. The social worker then went home immediately and brought him back a box of one hundred condoms. But my brother told her that he could not live without sex, that if he went without sex for too long he began to feel funny. He was unmoved when she asked him if he would like to have that done to him, someone infected with the HIV virus and knowing it having sex with him without telling him; perhaps he thought that is exactly what had happened to him. He was unmoved when she asked him if he would like someone to treat his sister (me) the way he had just treated that woman ("What if that had been your sister?"). He agreed to use the condoms in the future when she told him that HIV infection was dose-related, that is, the more of the virus you get, the more virus you have received, the quicker it kills you; if he wasn't telling people he was HIV-infected, perhaps they were not telling him if they were infected also; using a condom was not only to protect other people from him, it was also to protect himself from other people.

My brother told me that he could not go two weeks without having sex, he said it made him feel, and he lifted his shoulders up and then let them drop down; he looked sad, he looked defeated, but that did not stop me from saying cruelly, Every man I have ever known has said the same thing, two weeks without sex makes them feel funny. He had been trying to tell me that there was something unique about him, that he was an unusual person, a powerfully sexual man. Powerfully sexual men sometimes cause people to die right away with a bullet to the head, not first sicken and slowly die from disease. When we saw Dr. Ramsey for his checkup soon after we had this conversation, I told Dr. Ramsey in front of him about his sexual behavior and the risk he posed to other people and to himself; he *truupsed* and repeated that he could not go without sex for more than two weeks. He said he did not believe he had the HIV virus anymore and he demanded that Dr. Ramsey test him again. Dr. Ramsey reminded him that he had asked for a new test a few weeks before, after he had been released from the hospital and had gone for one of his checkups and had then said that he did not have AIDS and had been tested again and the results were positive. I now said that I would not pay for a new test, I was convinced that he was HIV-positive, so convinced that I had gotten myself into debt trying to save his life. He promised that he would try to be more careful, but as we were leaving, Dr. Ramsey said something which led my brother to know that as a hobby, he, Dr. Ramsey, served as a producer of many well-known Antiguan calypso singers. My brother got very excited when he heard this and said that he was a very good singer himself, such a good singer that when he sang women who heard him removed their clothes ("Me nar joke, mahn, when me sing, gahl a take ahff she clothes").

And I began again to wonder what his life must be like for him, and to wonder what my own life would have been like if I had not been so cold and ruthless in regard to my own family, acting only in favor of myself when I was a young woman. It must have been a person like this, men like this, men who are only urges to be satisfied, men who say they cannot help themselves, men who cannot save themselves, men who only know how to die, not at all how to live—it must have been such a man that my mother knew of when she communicated to me the grave danger to myself should I allow such a person to know me too well, communicated this to me so strongly that I grew up alienated from my own sexuality and, as far as I can tell, am still, to this day, not at all comfortable with the idea of myself and sex. And so too, it must be this sort of man that my brother was who accounts for the famous prudery that exists among a certain kind of Antiguan woman (the English-speaking West Indian woman, as far as I can tell; I do not know about the other women who speak the other languages). Such a woman will live for a long time; not so the Guianese girl who waited outside the gate for my brother to return from some outing or other.

Who is he? I kept asking myself. Who is he? How

does he feel about himself, what has he ever wanted? Girls to take off their clothes when they hear him sing? What could that mean? He doesn't make anything, no one depends on him, he is not a father to anyone, no one finds him indispensable. He cannot make a table, his father could make a table and a chair, and a house; his father was the father of many children. This compulsion to express himself through his penis, his imagination passing between his legs, not through his hands, is something I am not qualified to understand. One afternoon I had taken him to swim at a place where when I was a child many church picnics were held. It is now a beach with a hotel for tourists; he was swimming with my mother and they looked so beautiful, the water parted for them in ripplets, forming fat diagonal lines on either side of them, the two of them, one black, one gold, glistening, buoyant, happy just then, within speaking distance of each other but not speaking to each other at all. I could see them, I was standing on the sand, the beach, my children near me building structures out of the sand, structures that they had to protect from the waves since the tide was changing. This was my mother and this was my brother, my mother's youngest child, her last, and I can remember thinking at his birth (I was thirteen at the time) that his arrival marked a change in her, a change in her relationship to his father, a change in her relationship to the world. She became bitter, sharp; she and I quarreled all the time, she quarreled with everyone all the time. Her features collapsed, she was beautiful in the face before, really beautiful, everyone thought so, really thought so, even she did, but that wasn't true anymore after my brother was born. That afternoon they were swimming together; without speaking, they were swimming, still without speaking. My brother, seeing some European women who were swimming together and sharing conversation and laughter, swam up to them and said things that I could not hear and they responded with words that I could not hear. I don't know what they saw in him, this man so beautiful in the face, too thin in the body, but they indulged his flirtatiousness, perhaps enjoying this moment with a man they would have found dangerous in their own native surroundings just because of his complexion, this moment so free of friction, in the hot sun. And I don't know what he really saw in them, they were not beautiful in face or body, by the standards of

European or Other, or what he expected of them; it was only that he could not help himself, he had seen some women, he had made himself seen by them; the outcome would always be the same: sometimes women had sex with him, sometimes they didn't.

My mother came and sat next to me, and as we were sitting on the sand watching my children, my mother told me that God would bless me richly for bringing my brother the AZT, but I do not believe such a thing, because why would God suddenly enter into it now, when the time to have entered into it was to stop such a thing as this virus from occurring at all; and then my brother, too, came out of the water and he and my mother started to talk about how clever he was at growing things and my mother reminded him of "the fern." Not so very long ago, my mother paid a visit to Dominica, the place where she was born and where she lived until she was sixteen years of age, to see the last of her living relatives. Her mother, a Carib Indian of Dominica, is dead; her father, part Scot, part African, of Antigua, a policeman who emigrated to Dominica, is dead; her sister is dead, her brother is dead. The people she visited were related to her mother through various people I do not know, I have never met them. She had not been back to Dominica since years before I was born in 1949, and she did not say what made her want to return at that time. She had a wonderful visit, so she said, and while there and walking about, she found a fern that was unusual, something rare; she recognized it and she picked it up and put it in her bag, bringing it back to Antigua with her, where it throve quite happily in an old, leaky, white enameled chamber pot in a shady part of the yard. One day when my brother was in the most extreme grip of his drug addiction, he wanted some cocaine but had no money to buy some. He took my mother's fern and sold it. As she told me this, she laughed; he was sitting near her and she reached out to rub the top of his head; he *truupsed* and looked away, he was embarrassed; she meant to embarrass him, he and I knew this. He should not have taken her fern and sold it; I should not have been told about his selling the fern in just this way. I wanted to say to him, She doesn't know what she is doing, but I have never been able to say this to myself, I have never been able to forgive her for any of the things she did not know she was doing when she did them to me. I was looking at his face. She does not like memory, I wanted to tell him; you have no memory, I wanted to tell him, she taught you that. Some time before I was sixteen years of age, I might have taken a series of exams that, had I passed them, would have set me on a path that would have led me to be educated at a university, but just before all of that my mother removed me from school. There was no real reason for me to be removed from school, she just did it, removed me from school. My father was sick, she said, she needed me at home to help with the small children, she said. But no one would have died had I remained in school, no one would have eaten less had I remained in school; my brother would have been dead by now had this act of my mother's been all that remained of my life. Had my life stayed on the path where my mother had set it, the path of no university education, my brother would have been dead by now. I would not have been in a position to save his life, I would not have had access to a medicine to prolong his life, I would not have had access to money to buy the medicine that would prolong his life, however temporarily. And as we sat there, not face-to-face at all, she rubbing his head, telling humiliating stories about him, telling me some God or other would bless me, she did not remember this, she did not remember that if it had been up to her, I would not have been in a position to be blessed by any God, I might in fact be in the same position as my brother right now. When I was a child, I would hear her recount events that we both had witnessed and she would leave out small details; when I filled them in, she would look at me with wonder and pleasure and praise me for my extraordinary memory. This praise made an everlasting mark and nothing anyone could do made me lose this ability to remember, however selectively I remember. As I grew up, my mother came to hate this about me, because I would remember things that she wanted everybody to forget. I can see clearly even now the moment she turned on me with that razorlike ability to cut the ground out from beneath her children, and said I remembered too much ("You mine long, you know"). By then it was too late to tell me that.

That sun, that sun. On the last day of our visit its rays seemed as pointed and as unfriendly as an enemy's well-aimed spear. My mother cooked a delicious lunch for her grandchildren, a stew of corned beef from a tin with tomatoes and carrots and macaroni; they ate it so eagerly, as if they were starved, as if they could be called greedy. My brother said he would like to go for a walk with me alone. I was pleased by this and I also wondered what of mine he wanted; whenever he made a special point of being with me alone, it was to ask me for something I had that he wanted; earlier he had taken me aside to ask me for the pair of shorts that I was wearing; they were a pair of khaki shorts I usually wear when I go hiking in the mountains. I gave them to him, and even though I could easily replace them, I did not like giving them to him at all. I did not want them back, I wanted not to have had to give them in the first place. We walked up a road, past a monument to commemorate a slave who had led a revolt. The monument was surrounded by a steel fence and the gate was locked; the fence made of steel and the locked gate weren't meant to be a part of this particular commemoration to this slave's heroism. We walked past an old lighthouse. We walked past the place where my old school, an all-girls' school, used to stand. We walked past two ponds called Country Pond, and the origin of that name I do not know, but they have played a small, significant part in my own personal history: when I was about nine years old or so and a student at that same girls' school, the other girls thought of me as a bookish favorite of my teachers and as someone who could not defend herself, and was stuck-up; a particularly aggressive group of them would waylay me after school as I walked home and pin me to the ground while they took turns beating me up. There was no reason for it, I was not malicious, I was not a tattletale, I was not pretty. I was just very weak-looking, thin, and too tall for how thin I was. One day my mother, wondering why I was so late from school, came looking for me, saw from a distance a group of girls huddled over something lying on the ground, got closer, realized it was me, and gave the girl she found beating me an even worse beating. The girl's mother, on hearing about this, told my mother that she would set evil spirits on me and they would cause me to drown myself in one of these ponds. My mother did not doubt this girl's mother for one moment and I was immediately sent to visit my grandparents and aunt in Dominica, because it is well known that spirits cannot cross water, and in any case, the obeah practiced in Dominica was far superior to the kind practiced in Antigua. This began a long and painful separation from my family that ended when it became clear that I could not adjust very well to my mother's absence. When I returned, my second brother had already been born and the bitter, cruel mother I now know had just begun to take hold; the beautiful, intelligent person that I knew and this brother whom I was walking with was born too late to know, and when I described this person to him, this woman who read biographies of Florence Nightingale and Louis Pasteur, who knew all the symptoms of all the known tropical diseases, who knew about vitamin deficiencies and what foods could alleviate them, he thought it was something I was saying to amuse him, he thought I was making it up. I told him then, It is hard for us to leave our mother, but you are thirty years old, you are a grown man, you must leave; this one thing you should do before you die, leave her, find your own house as soon as you are well enough, find a job, support yourself, do this before you die. He said he understood what I was saying, he said that he had been thinking along the same lines. Earlier that day, my mother had told me of a plan she and he had to build another little room, right next to her bedroom, for him to live in. I did not say, You can't afford to do that, save that money for a time when it might be needed for medicine, taxi fares to the hospital, just save that money. I also did not say that my mother must have felt compelled to build my brother something at this time in his life: three months ago she was sure it would be a coffin. The room to be built would be small, the size of an ordinary tomb.

My brother and I walked up to the botanical gardens and found they were closed for repairs; they had been neglected for many years, many specimens had died, but now someone—most likely a Canadian, because they are so generous to the self-destructive of the world—a Canadian had given money to have the botanical gardens restored. We walked around the perimeter, and using a book on tropical botany that I carried and also relying on our own knowledge, we identified many plants. But then we came to a tree that we could not identify, not on our own, not from the book. It was a tree, only a tree, and it was either just emerging from a complete dormancy or it was half-dead, half-alive. My brother and I became obsessed with this tree, its bark, its leaves, its shape; we wondered where it was really from, what sort of tree it was. If it crossed his mind that this tree, coming out of a dormancy, a natural sleep, a temporary death, or just half-dead, bore any resemblance to him right then and there, he did not say, he did not let me know in any way. We walked on, past the botanical gardens, and we came upon some tamarind trees with ripe tamarinds on them; the tamarinds were hanging very high up on the trees and so my brother picked up stones and threw them at the fruits, hoping to knock some down, the way we would have done if we had been schoolchildren. He succeeded, we ate the tamarinds; they were not good, they were not bad, they were just tamarinds. We did not say anything then. We walked past the jail; he did not tell me if he had been in it, that time when he had been in trouble. He did not seem to notice it at all. We walked over to the grounds of his old school. It did not seem to have any memories for him; he noticed that it was dilapidated, he wondered why children were sent to a school with holes in the building. It was there he found the fruit of a mahogany tree, something we had both seen before, the fruit of a mahogany tree, but it was a marvel to us then, so perfectly shaped like a pear, the Northern Hemisphere fruit, not the avocado pear, but hard like the wood of the tree from which it comes. I brought it back to the Vermont climate with me and placed it on a windowsill, and one day when I looked, it had opened quietly, perfectly, into sections, revealing an inside that was a pink like a shell that had been buried in clean sand, and layers upon layers of seeds in pods that had wings, like the seeds of a maple. I did not know until then that the seeds of the mahogany tree were like that. We then walked past the Recreational Grounds, the public grounds where major public events are held. He pointed to a pavilion and told me that when he was a student at his school, he and a friend used to take girls under there and have sex ("Mahn, me used to bang up some girls under there"). We walked back to my mother's house.

I returned to my own home in Vermont with my children. I spoke to my brother, the one who was sick with HIV; I spoke to my brother, the middle one; I spoke to my mother. I never spoke to my oldest brother; there is no clear explanation for this, his story is another big chapter and he, too, can neither speak it nor write it down. My youngest brother, the sick one, had moved into the little room that had been built for him; my mother was very pleased that she had built it. He got stronger and stronger. Over the telephone my mother told me that he was very well, so well he might go to work; he found a job, but the person who had employed him ran out of money. He was better beyond anyone's expectation, he had gained quite a bit of weight, he was staying out all night, he was drinking beer, and when I asked if there was a certainty that there was only beer in the bottle, my mother was actually surprised that a beer bottle might have anything but beer in it; but immediately I heard he was drinking beer, I thought he would not stop at beer. He was seeing a lot of girls and presumably having sex with them; there was the Guianese girl and there were other girls, but no one ever said where those others came from. He and my mother had huge quarrels and unforgivable things were said, but after the quarrels were over, they would both feel that everything said had not really been meant.

One day a woman who, when we were little girls together, was my best friend called me on the telephone to tell me that some books I had given her had been stolen and could I replace them. She was in tears. I was very touched by this, because they were books I had written and when I had given them to her she did not seem particularly pleased to have them. We speculated about who might have taken them and why. Just as she was about to hang up, I asked her about my brother and she said he was quite well, he saw his friends, he was not working, he stayed out all night sometimes; he was drinking, he was never without a bottle of beer in his hand, there was always a girl waiting for him. She said his hair had gotten very thin. She said his lips had gotten red again. When I first saw him in the hospital, lying there almost dead, his lips were scarlet red, as if layers and layers of skin had been removed and only one last layer remained, holding in place the dangerous fluid that was his blood. His face was sharp like a carving, like an image embossed on an emblem, a face full of deep suffering, beyond regrets or pleadings for a second chance. It was the face of someone who had lived in extremes, sometimes a saint, sometimes a sinner.

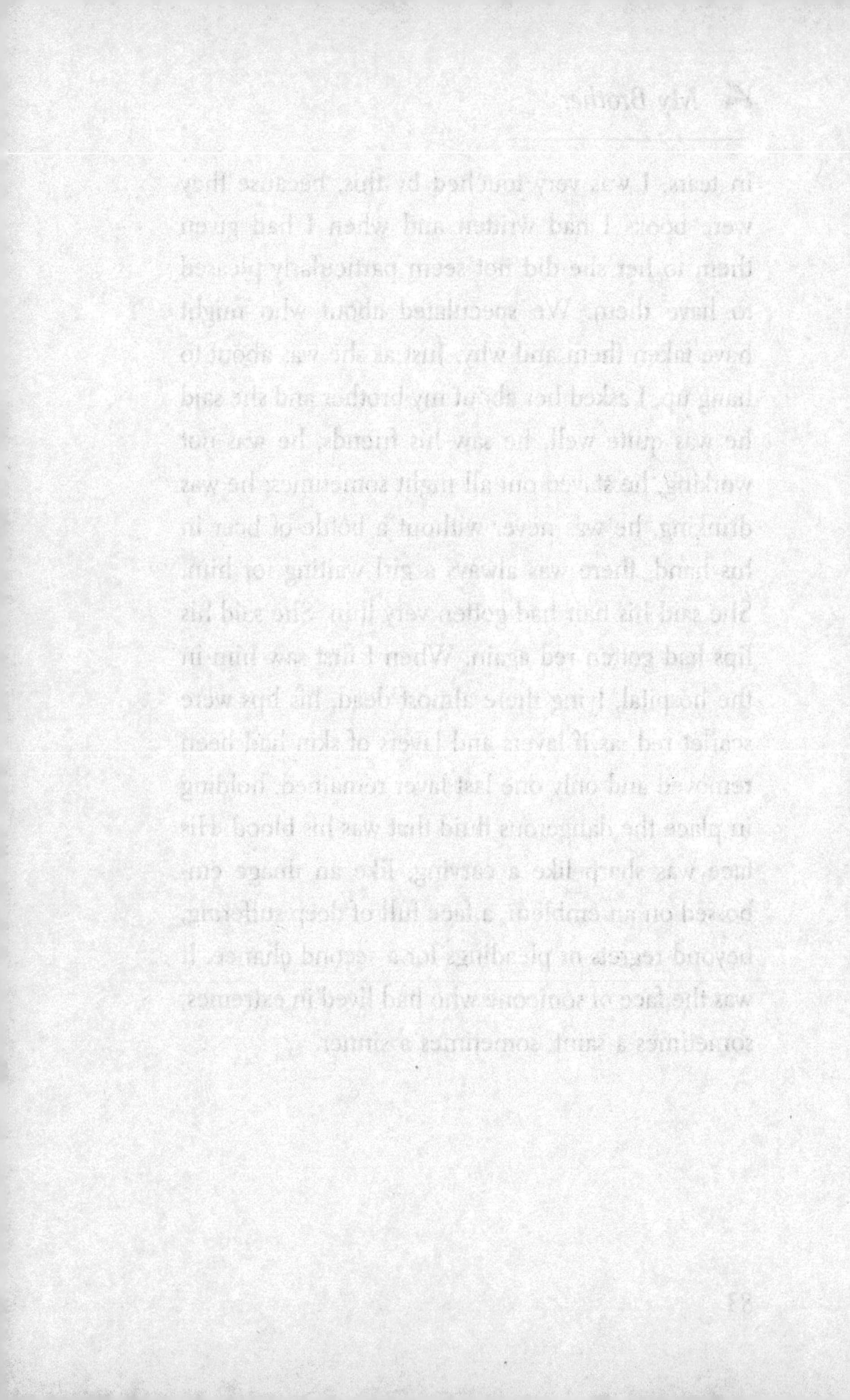

MY BROTHER DIED. I had expected him to, sometimes it seemed as if it would be a good thing if he were to just die. And then he did die. When he was still alive I used to try to imagine what it would be like when he was no longer alive, what the world would seem like the moment I knew he was no longer alive. But when that moment came, the moment I knew he was no longer alive, I didn't know what to think, I didn't know what to feel.

He had been dead for a long time. I saw him two months before he was actually dead. He was lying in his bed; his head was big, bigger than it used to be before he got sick, but that was because his body had become so small. The bed in which he lay dying I had bought for him. It was a small bed, a bed for a child. The sheets on the bed I had bought at Ames, a store in the small town in which I now live, a place he would never see. He would never see me in the place I now live, but I could see him in the place in which he was then living. He lived in death. Perhaps everyone is living in death, I actually do believe that, but usually it can't be seen; in his case it was a death I could see. He was alive, he could speak, he still breathed in and out, he still sometimes would demand a particular kind of food and then decide that he liked it or did not like it, but he wasn't alive in a way that I had ever seen anyone before. He was lying in his bed with the thin sheets on top of him, his eyes open, wide-open, as if they had been forced to be that way, his mouth open, as if it had been forced to be that way; he was lying in his bed, and yet he was somewhere else. When I saw him that time, the last time before he died, and he was lying in bed, his hands were invisible; they were beneath the sheets, the sheets were not moving up and down; his eyes were open and his mouth was open and his hands were not visible. And that was exactly the way he looked when the undertaker unzipped the plastic bag in which he lay when I went to see him at the undertaker's. When I saw him, though, lying in bed, two months before I saw him at the undertaker's, he was in his mother's house. She is my mother, too, but I wasn't talking to her then, and when I am not talking to her, she is someone else's mother, not mine. I could see him through the louvered windows while I was standing on the gallery. It was at the end of one of those days, like so many I used to know when I was a child, and that I wanted to run away from: in the east the darkness was already falling down from the sky; in the west, the sun, having exhausted itself from shining with such relentlessness, was hurrying to drop below the horizon. Not a bird sings then; chickens fly into trees to roost for the night, the trees become still; no one quarrels, people's voices are muted. It is not the usual time of day to be born or to die, it is the usual time of day to prepare to be born or to prepare to die; that was the time of day when I first saw him two months before he died. He did not die in the middle of that night.

When I was looking at him through the louvered windows, I was not thinking of myself in the sense of how it came to be that he was lying there dying and I was standing there looking at him. I was thinking of my past and how it frightened me to think that I might have continued to live in a certain way, though, I am convinced, not for very long. I would have died at about his age, thirty-three years, or I would have gone insane. And when I was looking at him through the louvered windows, I began to distance myself from him, I began to feel angry at him, I began to feel I didn't like being so tied up with his life, the waning of it, the suffering in it. I began to feel that it would be so nice if he would just decide to die right away and get buried right away and the whole thing would be done with right away and that would be that. I entered the house and stood in the doorway of the room in which he was lying. The house had a funny smell, as if my mother no longer had time to be the immaculate housekeeper she had always been and so some terrible dirty thing had gone unnoticed and was rotting away quietly. It was only after he was dead and no longer in the house and the smell was no longer there that I knew what the smell really was, and now as I write this, I cannot find a simile for this smell, it was not a smell like any I am familiar with. I stood looking at him for a long time before he realized I was there. And then when he did, he suddenly threw the sheets away from himself, tore his pajama bottoms away from his waist, revealing his penis, and then he grabbed his penis in his hand and held it up, and his penis looked like a bruised flower that had been cut short on the stem; it was covered with sores and on the sores was a white substance, almost creamy, almost floury, a fungus. When he grabbed his penis in his hand, he suddenly pointed it at me, a sort of thrusting gesture, and he said in a voice that was full of deep panic and deep fear, "Jamaica, look at this, just look at this." Everything about this one gesture was disorienting; what to do, what to say; to see my brother's grown-up-man penis, and to see his penis looking like that, to see him no longer able to understand that perhaps he shouldn't just show me—his sister—his penis, without preparing me to see his penis. I did not want to see his penis; at that moment I did not want to see any penis at all.

What I am writing now is not a journal; a journal is a daily account, an immediate account of what occurs during a certain time. For a long time after my brother died I could not write about him, I could not think about him in a purposeful way. It was really a short time between the time that he became sick and the time he died, but that time became a world. To make a world takes an eternity, and eternity is the refuge of the lost, the refuge for all things that will never be or things that have been but have lost their course and hope to recede with some grace, and even I believe this to be true, though I also know that I have no real way of measuring it.

His death was imminent and we were all anticipating it, including him, but we never gave any thought to the fact that this was true for all of us, too: our death was imminent, only we were not anticipating it . . . yet. Death was the thing that was going to happen to him, and yet every time I got on an airplane to go and pay him a visit, I was quite afraid that I would never come back: the plane would crash, or in some way not at all explainable, I would never come back.

There is a photograph of my brother in a book (an album) full of photographs collected by my husband. They are family photographs and they are in this book because my husband wanted to give our daughter a snapshot view of the first five years of her life. The photograph of my brother that is in this album shows a young man, beautiful and perfect in the way of young people, for young people are always perfect and beautiful until they are not, until the moment they just are not. In this photograph his skin is smooth; his skin looks as if it were a piece of precious fabric covering a soft surface (the structure that was his face), and if this fabric were to be forcefully pressed with the ball of a finger, it would eventually return to its smooth and shiny surface, looking untouched by experience of any kind, internal or external. He was beautiful then. He did unspeakable things then; at least he could not speak of them and I could not really speak of them to him. I could name to him the things he did, but he could not name to me the things he did. He stole from his mother (our mother, she was my own mother, too, but I was only in the process of placing another distance between us, I was not in the process of saying I know nothing of her, as I am doing now), he stole from his brothers; he would have stolen from me, too, but the things he could steal from me were not available to him: my possessions were stored on a continent far away from where he lived. He lied. He stole, he lied, and when I say he did unspeakable things, just what do I mean, for surely I know

I have lied and once I stole stationery from an office in which I worked. His unspeakable things were things he was unable to speak openly about. He could never say that anything in front of him was his own, or that anything in front of him came to him in a way that he did not find humiliating. He was a thief, he was not proud to say that most of what he had had come to him through stealing. In the place in which he lived when his skin was smooth and unblemished—he was really young then but beyond adolescence—he had some books on a shelf; they were school textbooks and one was a history of the West Indies, though really it was a history of the British West Indies. This book was a book he took from his school. I understood that, taking a book from school; when I was a little girl, living on that small island, I used to steal books from the library, not my school, but the library; the school that I attended had no books that I wanted to steal. I would not have wanted to steal a book about history; I stole only novels, and all the novels I stole were novels I had read, they were all written in the nineteenth century. I was not interested in history then, only so now; my brother had history books on his shelf. He was obsessed with the great thieves who had inhabited his part of the world, the great hero-thieves of English maritime history: Horatio Nelson, John Hawkins, Francis Drake. He thought that the thing called history was an account of significant triumphs over significant defeats recorded by significant people who had benefited from the significant triumphs; he thought (as do I) that this history of ours was primarily an account of theft and murder ("Dem tief, dem a dam tief"), but presented in such a way as to make the account seem inevitable and even fun: he liked the costumes of it, he liked the endings, the outcomes; he liked the people who won, even though he was among the things that had been won. But his life was real, not yet a part of history; his reality was that he was dead but still alive; his reality was that he had a disease called AIDS. And no matter what anyone says, or for that matter what anyone has discovered so far, it seems to me that to be so intimately acquainted with the organism that is the HIV virus is to be acquainted with death. We are all acquainted with death; each moment, each gesture, holds in it a set of events that can easily slide into realities that are unknown, unexpected, to the point of shock; we do not really expect these moments; they arrive and are resisted, denied, and then finally, inexorably, accepted; to have the HIV virus is to have crossed the line between life and death. On one side, there is life, and the thin shadow of death hovers over it; and on the other, there is death with a small patch of life attached to it. This latter is the life of AIDS; this was how I saw my brother as he lay in his bed dying.

I was in Miami, a city at the far southern end of North America, and ordinarily the word "Miami," representing this city, is familiar enough so that I can say it and know what I mean, and I can say it and believe that the person hearing it knows what I mean, but when I am writing all this about my brother, suddenly this place and the thing I am about to say seem foreign, strange. I was in Miami, and if someone asked me a question in regard to my family, I would make frank replies about my family and about my mother. It must have been wonderful in Miami then, but I will never really know, I can only repeat what other people said; they said that it was wonderful in Miami and they were glad to be there, or they wanted to be there. But I myself was in Miami, and I found Miami not to be in the tropical zone that I was from, and yet not in the temperate zone where I now live; Miami was in between, but its in-betweenness did not make me long for it. I missed the place I now live in, I missed snow, I missed my own house that was surrounded by snow, I missed my children, who were asleep or just walking about in the house surrounded by snow, I missed my husband, the father of my children, and they were all in the house surrounded by snow. I wanted to go home. One midday I left Miami, and when I left, it was warm and clear and the trip from Miami to Vermont should not have taken more than eight hours, but Miami is south and the farther north I got, the more temperate the weather turned and there were snowstorms which made air travel difficult and I arrived at my home in Vermont fourteen and one-half hours after I left Miami. In Miami I had taken a walk through the Fairchild Botanical Gardens, and while there I had bought two rhododendrons from New Guinea at the gift shop. The rhododendrons were in five-gallon pots and they were very awkward to carry on airplanes and through airport terminals. Perhaps I looked like a very sensible woman carrying two large plants covered with trumpet-shaped brilliant orange blooms in the middle of an airport and in the middle of January, because everyone I met was very kind and helped me with my plants and my various other traveling paraphernalia. I was so happy to reach my home, that is, the home I have now made for myself, the home of my adult life.

My two children were asleep in my son's bed. When I am away from home they like sleeping together. When I saw them asleep, breathing normally, their features still, they looked so beautiful, not doing anything that I felt was a danger to them or annoying to me, so that I did not have to call their name out loud, as if their name itself were a warning ("HAROLD," "ANNIE"), or as if their name itself held regret. I stood over them, looking down at them and thinking how much I loved them and how glad I was that I had them, and I bent over and kissed them and they woke up and were glad to see me and begged me to get into bed with them and snuggle with them until they fell asleep again. I got into bed with them, meaning to stay there only until they fell asleep, but I fell asleep also; I awoke because my husband woke me up.

It was six o'clock in the morning, the winter daylight was still mostly silver, it had in it only a little bit of yellow, it had in it only a little bit of pink, I could see this as I left my son's room, standing in the hallway and facing a window.

When my husband woke me up, he said, "Sweetie, come, come, I have to talk to you" (that is just the way he said it). In the dark of the room I could see his face; that isn't really possible, to see something like a face in the dark of a room, but it is true all the same, I could see his face. It was an anxious face, a troubled face; on his face I could see that he was worried about something and I thought that something was himself. I said to him, "What's the matter?" I asked him, "What's wrong?" (and in just that way, using just those words). He would only reply, "Come, come, I have to talk to you." In the hall where I could see the silvery daylight with just a little pink and just a little yellow, he said, "Dalma just called, Devon died." And when he said "Devon died" I thought, Oh, it's Devon who died, not one of his relatives, not someone of his, this is not someone *he* has to grieve for. I was so glad about that, so glad at the thought, the feeling that this death, this look of sadness in his face, had to do with someone who was not related to him. He was not going to suffer a grief. My husband is someone I love; it is a love I had not expected or even really knew existed; I would rather bad things or unpleasant things happen to me. I can't bear to see him suffer; in any case, he takes suffering too seriously, too hard; it is better when bad things are happening to me, then I don't have to worry about him. And then again, I believe that I am better at handling bad things than he.

I got the children ready for school and gave them breakfast. I told them their uncle had died. They were not surprised, they had been expecting it; they would go to the funeral, they would go swimming with our friends Bud and Connie; Bud and Connie would take them to the Lobster Pot for dinner. I took the children to the bus stop, I had a nice chat with the other mothers while we waited for the bus to come, I did not tell them that my brother had died. I returned home, I called the travel agent and made travel arrangements; I sat and waited for a woman from a newspaper who wanted to ask me questions about a book I had written and had just published. This woman came and she asked me all sorts of questions about my past and my present, about the way in which I had become a writer, about the way in which my life, with its improbable beginning (at least from the way it looks to someone else now) of poverty and neglect, cruelty and humiliation, loss and deceit, had led to a sure footing in the prosperous and triumphant part of the world, leading to her, a newspaper reporter, being interested in my life. Whatever questions she asked me about anything, it was easy to be without mercy and to answer truthfully: about my mother, about the reasons for no longer wanting to associate my writing with the magazine where I had developed my skills as a writer. For the magazine I wrote for all of my writing life so far was like the place in which I had grown up; it was beautiful, an ideal of some kind, but it had been made vulgar and ugly by the incredibly stupid people who had become attracted to it. I said nothing about the death of my brother, which had actually occurred hours before (though really he had been dead for at least a year before the breath left his body), I had vowed to tell her nothing about my brother and his illness and now his death. If I had spoken to her while he was just sick and even almost dying (though he was in a state of almost dying for a long time), I would not have hesitated to tell her about my brother's illness, to tell her of his impending death (and also to bring up the fact that all of us face impending death). I could not speak to her of his just dying. I could not make sense of it just then. His death was so surprising, even though I had been expecting it; it hung in front of me, not like a black cloud but like a block of something hard and cold and impenetrable. I spoke to her and I spoke to her, she asked me questions and she asked me questions. All the things I said to her were true, all the things I said to her were filled with meaning. The day was cold, it was the middle of January, the sun was shining. For me such a thing is a paradox: the sun is shining, yet the air is cold. And as I was talking to this woman from the newspaper who kept asking me questions and questions and whose questions I kept answering and answering, I looked out a window and I saw that an animal, a deer, had eaten up some especially unusual evergreens that my friend Dan Hinkley had sent to me from his nursery in Kingston, Washington. And the sight of the evergreens, all eaten up in a random way, not as if to satisfy a hunger but to satisfy a sense of play, suddenly made me sad, suddenly made me wish that this, my brother dying, had not happened, that I had never become involved with the people I am from again, and that I only wanted to be happy and happy and happy again, with all the emptiness and meaninglessness that such a state would entail.

I was walking up and down the floor of my kitchen, the floor was pine, a type of wood that reminded me of my father, who was a carpenter. This man was my brother's real father and not really my own, my father was someone else I did not know, I knew only this man and to me he was my father. He was a man I loved and had known very well, better than his own children knew him (my brother who was dead, my brother who was a merchant in the market on Saturdays, my brother who had almost killed our mother when he threw her to the ground while trying to prevent her from throwing stones at him). My brother's coffin was made of that kind of wood, pine; my other brother, the one who is a merchant in the market on Saturdays, had picked it out. It cost the least of all the kinds of coffins that were on sale at the undertaker's, I paid for it with traveler's checks. As a child I was afraid of the undertaker, Mr. Straffee; as a child, all the furniture I came in contact with was made of this wood, pine: the chair that I sat on at home, the floor that I walked on at home, the bed

I slept in, the table on which my mother would place the meal I ate in the middle of a schoolday, my desk at school, the chair I sat on behind the desk at school—all of it was made from this wood, pine. The floor on which I stood that morning that my brother had died was cold and the planks had pulled away a little from each other.

I called all the doctors who had prescribed medicines for my brother to tell them he had died. Their names were Scattergood, Hart, and Pillemer. Only when I had called them, standing by the telephone, did their names stand out to me, as if their names had drawn me to them all along. They said how sorry they were to hear of it. I called the pharmacist to tell him that my brother had died. His name was Ed. He had been very kind and sympathetic, often trusting that I would pay him the hundreds and sometimes thousands of dollars' worth of medicine that I had charged; no matter how much I owed him, he always gave me the medicines that had been prescribed to ease my brother's suffering and prolong his life. I went to the grocery store in the little village to buy something, and when I told Pete, the grocer, that my brother had died, he told me how sorry he was and he said that he was sure that his wife, Debby, would be sorry to hear it, too. Everyone I told that my brother had just died said how sorry they were, they would say this, "I'm sorry," and those two words became so interesting to hear: everyone tried to say them with an emphasis that they hoped would convey the sincerity of their feelings; they really were sorry that this person they did not know was dead, that this person they would not have liked at all (I knew this, for they would have found him charming, he was so good-looking, he could remember to have good manners when it suited him, when he wanted to get something, but really in the end he would have found their devotion to the routine, the ordinariness of pure, hard work, devoid of satisfaction, yet he would not have quarreled with them, he would only have done everything he knew how to accentuate to them the futility, the emptiness of the thing called life, the thing called living—they would not have liked him). But these words, "I'm sorry," which sometimes are said with a real depth of feeling, with true sincerity, sometimes just out of politeness, are such a good thing to hear if you are in need of hearing them, and just then I was in need of hearing those words, "I'm sorry," "I am so sorry."

I did not love my brother, I did not like my brother, I was only so sorry that he had died, I was comforted to hear other people say that they were sorry that he had died. And I was full of admiration for the people who could say this: "I'm sorry," for they said it with such ease, they said it as if they were only breathing.

When I saw him for the last time still alive, though he looked like someone who had been dead for a long time and whose body had been neglected, left to rot—when I had last seen him and he was still alive, I had quarreled with him. I had gone to see him one weekend, leaving my family to spend the Thanksgiving holiday by themselves. My brother, the one who is a merchant on Saturdays in the market, had called to say Devon was not doing very well, Devon was sinking, Devon was going down. That was just the way he said it: not doing very well, sinking, going down. For the sickeningly floriferous thrush growing in his throat, a doctor had prescribed something; the pharmacist placed thirty tablets of it into a bottle so small I could hide it in the palm of my hand and the bottle could not be detected; the bottle of that medicine cost so much that I could not pay for it then; nor could I pay for the other medicines I needed, medicines for pain, not medicines to ease pain but medicines to make you not feel anything at all. I could not pay for any of it with cash, I could pay for it only with credit; and in that way, though not solely in that way, his illness and death reminded me again and again of my childhood: this living with credit, this living with the hope that money will come reminded me of going to a grocer whose name was Richards, not the one who was a devout Christian whom later we went to, for the grocers named Richards, whether they had religious conviction or not, charged us too much anyway and then forced us to pay our debts no matter how unable my parents were to do so; my parents had more children than they could afford to feed, but how were they to know how much food or disease, or anything in general, would cost, the future never being now; only it actually comes, the future, later.

And when I saw my brother for the last time, alive, in that way he was being alive (dead really, but still breathing, his chest moving up and down, his heart beating like something, beating like something, but what, but what, there was no metaphor, his heart was beating like his own heart, only it was beating barely), I was so tired of him being in this state, not alive, not dead, but constantly with his demands, in want, constantly with his necessities, weighing on my sympathy, at times preying on my sympathy, whichever way it fell, I was sick of him and wanted him to go away, and I didn't care if he got better and I didn't care if he died. That was just the way I felt, that was the only thing I felt just at that moment when he would not die and when he would not live; I only wanted him to do one or the other and then leave me alone.

I did not kiss him goodbye when I was returning home to my family, I did not give him a goodbye hug. I said to him at the end of my visit (four days), Goodbye, and he said, So this is it, no hug no nothing? (and he said it in that way, in conventional English, not in the English that instantly reveals the humiliation of history, the humiliations of the past not remade into art); and I said, Yes, this is it, goodbye, and perhaps I will see you again, and I was aware that when I said it—perhaps I will see you again—I was assuming something that was not true at all: seeing him again was left to me, seeing him again was something that I could decide. I did not feel strong, I felt anger, my anger was everything to me, and in my anger lay many things, mostly made up of feelings I could not understand, feelings I might not ever understand, feelings that everyone who knows me understands with an understanding that I will never know, or that someone who has never met me at all would understand as if they had made up my feelings themselves.

Two months before I saw him alive for the last time, there had been a big hurricane, and then weeks later a smaller one. The first one raged over the island for thirty-six hours and caused the usual destruction that goes with a hurricane, but what people talked about afterward was the sound of the wind and the rain; it sounded as if someone were being killed and the someone being killed was screaming "Murder! Murder!" My brother could only lie in his bed. He heard that sound that seemed to be someone saying "Murder! Murder!" He must have heard the sound of large trees crashing into houses, water flooding the streets, the poles holding up the wires that carried electricity splitting, then hitting the ground. When the poles that held the wires carrying electricity hit the ground, the house in which my brother lay, his mother's house, our mother's house, became dark and then filled with a light that had been absent for many years; for my mother got out the old kerosene lamps and lighted them. The light of the kerosene lamp was the only light I knew at night when I was a child.

Everyone inside the house was frightened; they could hear the disaster of the hurricane affecting other people in a dramatic way: dwellings being ripped apart, children crying, people calling in panic, in fear, certainly not in joy, certainly not in welcome. In that room, inside that house, my brother lay still, while outside it was not still at all, and what did he say, what did he think, what did he feel? He felt nothing, he said, he heard the noise of the wind and the rain, he did not hear the people; the light from the kerosene lamp only made him wonder ("De noise bad, man, but me no pay it no mind; dem people, dem people, me a warn you, deh no good, deh no good; de light you know, 'e like dem old-time days"). And in that moment (and by moment I mean a length of time that does not correspond to a scientific definition, and by moment again, I do not mean just a figure of speech) I felt (and perhaps incorrectly, but all the same these are my thoughts on his dying and on his life—and that is one of the reasons to outlive all the people who can have anything to say about you, not letting them have the last word) that I understood him again—nothing new, an old insight, this one—that he was a dreamer, that he liked events best when he could be in them but not have them ask anything of him, that he could observe and have the sensation of something, but while doing so he must not be expected to save himself or anyone else. I remembered then being with him for the first time after twenty years, and lying on his bed in his old shack of a house, the little one-room house that was the house I had grown up in; it had seemed so big to me when I was a child, I lived in it with my mother (the woman who later also became his mother) and my father (the man who really was his father and really was not mine), and I was very happy in it when I was a small child, and then I was very unhappy in that house when I was growing out of my childhood, and my unhappiness in that house coincided with his birth and the birth of the two other boys (my brothers and his brothers) who were born just before him; and so that time (1986 in January) when I saw him again for the first time after twenty years, I was lying in his bed and he was sitting in the doorway speaking to a friend of his, they were planning a career, or something like a career in Dub music, and they were both smoking marijuana, which they did not call marijuana; they called it the Weed, as if that name, the Weed, made it something harmless, something not to be taken seriously. They laughed at me when I told them not to smoke so much marijuana, and then they started to smoke cocaine. And later, as my brother lay dying in his mother's house, I ran into this boy, his friend, as I was visiting my other brother who sells things at the market, whom I was helping sell things in the market, and this boy, my dying brother's old friend, came up to us to buy some soda, and he had with him a woman and a child, not his wife, just the mother of his child. The three of them were together and they were a family and they looked so very nice, like a picture of a family, healthy and prosperous and attractive, and also safe. This old friend of my brother's did not recognize me, and so I reminded him of how I knew him, and even so, he didn't ask after my brother, and even when I told him in a quite frank way about my brother's condition, it didn't seem to interest him at all, and I urged him to visit his old friend and he said he would, but he never did, he never did at all.

When I was lying on his bed that time in 1986, I was looking up at the ceiling; the little house was then old, or at least it looked old; the beams in the roof were rotting, but in a dry way, as if the substance of the wood was slowly being drawn out of it, and so the texture of the wood began to look like material for a sweater or a nightgown, not something as substantial as wood, not something that might offer shelter to many human beings. Looking up at the roof then, rotting in that drying-out way, did not suggest anything to me, certainly not that the present occupant of the house, my brother, might one day come to resemble the process of the decaying house, evaporating slowly, drying out slowly, dying and living, and in living looking as if he had died a very long time ago, a mummy preserved by some process lost in antiquity that can only be guessed at by archaeologists.

As I lay there I could hear our mother busy outside. In a climate like ours we live outside. When I was a child and my mother was trying to teach me European table manners, this was done inside, with the three of us—my mother, my father, and me—sitting at a table that he, my father (that man I knew so well, better than his own children—and that was how I came to know him so well, I was not really his child) had made, they both approving of the way I managed knife and fork and food, and my mouth all properly arranged. All things foreign were done inside, all things familiar and important were done outside; and this was true even of sleep, for though we fell asleep inside the house, as soon as the eyes were closed and sleep came on, no one stayed inside, all dreams, or so it seemed to me, took place outside; and in any case, as soon as we woke up, the first thing was to observe the outside of our house to make sure it had stayed the same as when we last saw it the night before. But at that moment, again in 1986, when I was lying inside the house in which my brother was living, my mother was outside talking to herself, or to a chicken that got in her way, or to the cats she had adopted which were just recovering from fish poisoning, as was my mother, but the cats were lagging in their recovery. Our mother—and sometimes I think of her as my mother only, and then sometimes she is the mother of my brothers also, and when she's our mother, she's another entity altogether—had recovered almost at the same moment she became sick from eating some fish, grouper, that must have fed on something poisonous in the sea and had sickened everyone and everything that had eaten it. A dog got in her way and she cursed him; my brother's friend got in her way, she cursed him and he laughed; she cursed my brother and he laughed. I did not get in her way, I was inside on the bed lying down, but in any case, I no longer got in her way, I had removed myself from getting in her way, I was in a position in my own life that did not allow for getting in my mother's way, she could not curse me, I no longer needed her. Even so, I still ate the food she cooked, and that was what she was busy outside doing then: cooking some food for me. She was a very good cook; I did not like her cooking when I was a child, but when I was lying in my brother's bed I loved all the food she cooked, all the food I would not eat as a child: fungi, saltfish with antroba (eggplant), breadfruit, doukona. I longed for these foods and was so glad to have them cooked for me, and not just cooked for me but cooked for me by her. It was while my brother was ill and I began to visit him (I did not take care of him, I only visited him and took him medicines, his mother took care of him) that I decided not to eat any food she cooked for me, or accept any food she offered me at all. It was not a deliberate decision, it was not done in anger. My brother, the one who sells food in the market, the one who had stopped speaking to my mother even though he lived in the same house as she, cooked his own food and would not let her cook anything for him and would not eat anything she cooked no matter how hungry he was. He did not like his mother anymore, he did not love his mother anymore. He called her Mrs. Drew, the name that ordinary people called her, just that, Mrs. Drew; he called her only, used her name only when he could not avoid it, when to address her without speaking her name would cause attention to be drawn to himself (someone might wonder, Why does he not speak to his mother directly?). My brother who was dying (and he was dying; there were times when he seemed sick, just sick, but mostly he was just dying), he too before he got sick called her only Mrs. Drew, but as the life of his death overwhelmed him, he came to call her Mother, and then only Muds. "Muds," he would say, "Muds." At that point in his life, that moment in 1986 when I was lying on his bed, looking up at the beams of his ceiling that would eventually remind me of his dry, rotting, shriveling body, he too no longer ate the food she cooked; this was part of a separation he wished to make between himself and his family. It was at this time that he proclaimed himself a Rastafarian and spoke constantly of Jah. The impulse was a good one, if only he could have seen his way to simply moving away from her to another planet, though perhaps even that might not have been far enough away.

And so I stopped eating my mother's food, inspired by the acts of two of my three brothers, who were much younger than I (by eleven and thirteen years). In my case, my case of not eating the food my mother provided for me, this act was full of something, I do not know what, but this occurred to me long after I was in the midst of doing it: that just as I was deciding not to eat my mother's food anymore, and thinking (and feeling) that this decision was really a decision to rid myself of a profoundly childish attachment to her, I was only reliving a memory, for when I was a child I would not eat the food my mother cooked. When I was a very small child, I would eat food only if she chewed it first; then I must have outgrown that, because I remember the difficulty I had with eating was in eating anything she cooked at all. And so not eating food my mother cooked for me as a sign of distancing myself from her was a form of behavior I had used a long time ago, when I felt most close to and dependent on her.

When my father died (this man who was not my real father; my real father eventually died also, but I did not know him and his life and death do not at all concern me, except when I am visiting the doctor and my medical history becomes of interest), I had been living away from my family for ten years. I learned of his death three months after he had died and been buried. My mother and I were in one of our periods of not speaking to each other, not on the telephone, not in letters. In the world I lived in then, my old family was dead to me. I did not speak of them, I spoke of my mother, but only to describe the terrible feelings I had toward her, the terrible feelings she had toward me, in tones of awe, as if they were exciting, all our feelings, as if ours had been a great love affair, something that was partly imaginary, something that was partly a fact; but the parts that were imaginary and the parts that were only facts were all true. She did not like me, I did not like her; I believe she wanted me dead, though not actually; I believe I wanted her dead, though not really. When my father died and she wrote to tell me three months later, I could not have known that such a thing, the death of this man, would make me feel as if I could not be moved from the place I was in when I read of his death. I had received the letter just before the onset of the Christmas season, and it made a time when I was always unhappy even more so. I had many friends, but they were not my family, they were only my friends; they had their own families, I was not their family. I wept. I did not think I should die, too, not consciously, not unconsciously.

In the letter telling me that my father (that is, the man who was not really my father but whom I thought of as my father, and the man who had filled that role in my life) had died, my mother said that his death had left them impoverished, that she had been unable to pay for his burial, and only the charitable gifts of others had allowed him to have an ordinary burial, not the extraordinary burial of a pauper, with its anonymous grave and which no proper mourners attend. The letter was not designed to make me feel guilty. My mother did not know of such a concept, guilt outside a court of law, feelings of guilt resulting from accusations made among ordinary people in their lives as lived day to day; she only knew of guilt as it existed in a court of law, with its formality of accusation and deliberation and then judgment. To her, she had simply described the reality of her situation, but I felt condemned because I had so removed myself from my family that their suffering had gone unnoticed by me, and even as I wept over my father's death, I would not have done much to prevent it, and even as I wept over my father's death and my mother's description of emotional pain and financial deprivation, I would not do a thing to alleviate it. It was ten years after I left my home that he died, it was ten years after he died before I saw my home again, and among the first things I wanted to do was to see the place in the graveyard where he was buried. But no one wanted to take me there; my mother said that since they had not bought the plot, most likely by then someone else was buried in it, for a plot was reused if it had not been bought by the family of the dead within seven years' time. The grave had never had a tombstone; no one in his family had visited his grave since the day of his funeral.

And so one day during the time when my brother was dying, I insisted that my mother and I pay a visit to the cemetery in which my father had been buried; I had the sentimental notion that perhaps my brother could be buried nearby, as near as possible to his own father. We passed through the door of that Dead House, she and I together, and as we did so, my own complicated and contradictory feelings about the dead came up and lay on the ground before my feet, and each step I took forward they moved forward, too, like a form of shadowing; all my feelings about the dead, determinedly unresolved and beyond me to resolve, lay at my feet, moving forward when I moved forward, again like a form of shadowing. The dead never die, and I now say this—the dead never die—as if it were new, as if no one had ever noticed this before: but death is like that (I can see); it happens every day, but when you see mourners, they behave as if it were so new, this event, dying—someone you love dies

—it has never happened before; it is so unexpected, so unfair, unique to you. The dead never die, let me just say it again.

She and I, I and my mother, walked through the graveyard looking for my father's, her husband's, grave, the place he had been buried, the plot, but she could not remember where it might have been. It was not in the place where Anglicans are buried, or the place where Catholics are buried, or the place where Moravians are buried; it might have been in the place where Methodists are buried, for when he was born he had been christened a Methodist, but when he died he was no longer a practicing Methodist (he was no longer a practicing anything, really, by the time he died), and because my mother had no money to pay for a burial, the Methodist minister would not bury him for free. My mother and I walked up and down in the graveyard looking for his grave; she thought it might be near a tree, she remembered a tree, but there were many trees in the graveyard; she stood at many angles trying to remember where it might be, what she could see the moment his coffin was being lowered into the ground, but she could not remember. She did know that he was buried in the part of the cemetery reserved for people who were not Anglicans, not Methodists, not Moravians, not Catholics, just people who belonged to the other Christian sects, only she did not know where. She was wearing a blue skirt, a blue that is the color of seawater, Caribbean seawater when it is seen from far away; I cannot remember the color of her blouse, and this must be why: as we were walking about, going to and fro, looking down at the ground, we could hear lizards scurrying around in the dry brush that surrounded us; the graveyard looked like everything else in a place like that, as soon as you turn your back, everything will collapse into a state of dry decay; she and I stopped walking and we were just standing still when suddenly a lizard came over to my mother and leaped up the front of her skirt and started climbing as if it were bent on scaling all the way up her front. She did not shriek and run away, as I would have done if this had happened to me; instead, she stood there and shook the lizard off her, not in a calm way, not in a frenzy, not with fear, just in her way, she shook the lizard off. As she shook the lizard off, she said that she hoped it wasn't one of those people, meaning the dead, come to tell her something that would make her want to join them ("Eh-eh, me ah wahrn you, dem people no get me, you know"), and she said this with a laugh. It all happened so quickly that I did not have time to shriek and run away, which is what I feel I want to do each time I remember this; I was not full of calm, I was not full of frenzy or full of fear; I am only all of these things at once each time I remember this.

It was on this visit that I began to speak of my mother in the old way, the way I did before I had written of my life with her, in a voice of awe, as if I, even I, could not believe the things I was saying, could not believe I really knew such a person. When I told my husband about the lizard, he said, "Really?" and he smiled as he said it, and I wondered if I seemed to be telling a tale, like a child in books I used to read when I was a child, or like a child in some of the books I now read to my own children. To "Really?" I would reply, "Yes, yes, really!" This, too, did happen: inside the house, my brother was slowly evaporating; outside, everything was itself, not orderly, not disorderly, just itself. I was watching my mother do something ordinary, scale some fish under a tree, but then I noticed that the tree, which used to be a soursop tree, was no longer itself; all that remained of it was its charred trunk. In my now privileged North American way (my voice full of pity at the thought of any kind of destruction, as long as my great desires do not go unmet in any way), I asked my mother what had happened to the tree, and she, without paying any real attention to me, told me that the tree had become a nuisance to her and so she had set fire to it and burned it down. And it is in this way that the tree became a nuisance to her: My mother had gone to visit some of her remaining relatives in Dominica, the ones who were not dead and were still speaking to her. While there, she ate a passion fruit and its flavor so pleased her that she pocketed its seeds, and when she returned to Antigua, she planted them and they grew with such vigor that they outgrew their first support, a trellis made of a bedstead and corrugated galvanize, and then leaped up into the soursop tree, which grew weak from this burden. The weakened soursop tree then became attractive to a colony of parasitic insects, and while living in the soursop tree the parasitic insects prospered and multiplied; this was not surprising at all, it was predictable. The parasitic insects, in their comfort and prosperity, expanded and began to infest the house. My mother tried to contain them with insecticides (imported from North America), insecticides with ingredients so toxic they are unavailable to consumers in North America. The parasitic insects could not be contained, they could not be eradicated, and that was what my mother wanted, that the parasitic insects should be eradicated. Her impulse is not unheard-of, the desire to eradicate all the things that are an annoyance, all the things that interfere with the smooth running of your day, a day which should produce for you a feeling of complete satisfaction, a kind of happiness even; such a desire appears quite normal, it even has historical precedence. The parasitic insects would not go away, and so one day she doused their source, the soursop tree, with kerosene and set it alight. The soursop tree burned; its parasitic partner, the passion-fruit vine, burned also. I was not there to witness this inferno, the burning of tree and vine and parasitic insects. But I was plunged into despair, for I recognized again that the powerful sense my mother has of herself is not something I had imagined and I was grateful that only a soursop tree, a passion-fruit vine, and some insects had gotten in its path. It's possible that in another kind of circumstance the shape of the world might have been altered by her presence. But this woman, my mother, had only four people to make into human beings.

I did not see the soursop tree and its parasites (passion fruit, insects) perish in the blaze my mother caused; I could only imagine it. Much time after it had occurred, a lone seedling of a passion fruit sprang up just outside the gate that separated my mother's house from the street. It grew to about eighteen inches tall, it lasted at just that height for a long time; after the hurricane occurred and when I saw my brother for the last time, I noticed that the passion fruit no longer existed. So much was occurring at the time I noticed this, the absence of the passion fruit's existence, that I could only notice it, not attach any significance to it, but there is significance to it all the same. And from the place I could look down at the stunted passion fruit—for it was that, stunted, unable to go on, unable to go back, it could not yet die—I could no longer see the soursop tree, I could no longer see the remains of its charred trunk, only the blue sky above it. I could only imagine it below that blue sky, an innocent sky, a sky that looked as if nothing important had ever taken place beneath it. But a glance away from the charred soursop trunk is where my mother's old stone heap used to be, and it was in this place that once my brother's and my life intersected, and this now has a meaning only because my own life can make it have one. At that moment in my mother's life, when her youngest child, my brother who was dying, was born, my mother's life (a life she might have had in mind, or a life that had become a nightmare; how could I, how can I know) collapsed (I could feel that then, I can see it now). Her husband (the man who was not really my own father, my brother's real father) was old and sickly and they could not properly support the family they had made. I was always being asked to forgo something or other that had previously occupied my leisure time, and then something or other that was essential (my schooling), to take care of these small children who were not mine. At thirteen, at fourteen, at fifteen, I did not like this, I did not like my mother's other children, I did not even like my mother then; I liked books, I liked reading books, I did not like anything else as much as I liked reading a book, a book of any kind. My youngest brother was two years old when one day he was left in my charge, my mother placed him in my care while she ran errands; perhaps I knew what these errands were, but I no longer do, I cannot remember what it was she had to do and so left me alone to care for him. Mr. Drew, our father (though his father, not really mine), was not at home. But I liked reading a book much more than I liked looking after him (and even now I like reading a book more than I like looking after my own children, but looking after my own children is something I cannot describe in terms of liking or anything else), and even then I would have said that I loved books but did not love him at all, only that I loved him because I was supposed to and what else could I do. All day I was left to look after him, and all day, instead of doing so, I read a book, a book whose title and plot or anything else about it I cannot remember just now. The day must have passed in the same rhythm as the pace with which I turned the pages (and I recognize this way of phrasing this event as romantic, even literary, for the day must have passed with its own usualness and did not care about me in particular or in general), and so when I finished reading the book I realized the day was ending and my mother would soon return home.

Between my coming to the end of the book and the time my mother should return home there were not many minutes remaining, only minutes were left for the chores that should have taken me an entire day to complete. I did the things I thought my mother would notice immediately; changing my brother's diaper was not among them. This was the first thing my mother noticed, and only now I can say (because I can see) "Of course." My brother, the one who was dying, who has died, who while dying could not take himself to the bathroom and freely control his bowel movements, then as a little boy, two years old, wore diapers and needed to have someone change them from time to time when they grew soiled. That day (and I cannot remember if it was a Monday, a Tuesday, or a Wednesday, but I do know with certainty that it was not a Saturday or a Sunday) when I had been reading instead of taking care of him, I did not notice that in his diaper was a deposit of my brother's stool, and by the time my mother returned from her errands—and she did notice it—the deposit of stool had hardened and taken the shape of a measure of weight, something used in a grocery store or in the fish market or the meat market or the market where only ground provisions are sold; it was the size of that measure signifying a pound. And in it, this picture of my brother's hardened stool, a memory, a moment of my own life is frozen; for his diaper sagged with a weight that was not gold but its opposite, a weight whose value would not bring us good fortune, a weight that only emphasized our family's despair: our fortunes, our prospects were not more than the contents of my brother's diaper, and the contents were only shit. When my mother saw his unchanged diaper, it was the realization of this that released in her a fury toward me, a fury so fierce that I believed (and this was then, but even now many years later I am not convinced otherwise) that she wanted me dead, though not in a way that would lead to the complications of taking in my actual existence and then its erasure, for she was my mother, my own real mother, and my erasure at her own hands would have cost her something then; my erasure now, my absence now, my permanent absence now, my death now, before her own, would make her feel regal, triumphant that she had outlived all her inferiors: her inferiors are her offspring. She mourns beautifully, she is admirable in mourning; if I were ever to be in mourning, this is the model, the example, I would imitate. At that stage of my life I was fifteen, my brother was two years old—I was unable to help her make sense of her life. The man she had married was sick and could not really build houses anymore, he could not really make furniture anymore; she might have loved him for a moment, she might have loved him for many moments, I never knew, but there was a child almost two years old, there was a child almost four years old, there was a child almost six years old. These were all his children. I was not his child, I was not a part of the real debacle of her life, and then again, worst of all, I could not help her out of it. I insisted on reading books. In a fit of anger that I can remember so well, as if it had been a natural disaster, as if it had been a hurricane or an erupting volcano, or just simply the end of the world, my mother found my books, all the books that I had read, some of them books I had bought, though with money I had stolen, some of them books I had simply stolen, for once I read a book, no matter its literary quality I could not part with it. (I then had no sense of literary quality, literary quality being a luxury, luxury being absent from my existence unless I saw an illustration of what this might be on a tin of cheap powder imported from England, and this picture of luxury only demonstrated what it might look like if one did not have to work at all, and so luxury was presented as contempt for working and any association with the dullness of the everyday.) A cauldron of words, even a world perhaps, may have passed, but not between us, though by then it would have been only one way, for I could make no response. But there was a moment when in a fury at me for not taking care of her mistakes (my brother with the lump of shit in his diapers, his father who was sick and could not properly support his family, who even when well had made a family that he could not properly support, her mistake in marrying a man so lacking, so lacking) she looked in every crevice of our yard, under our house, under my bed (for I did have such a thing and this was unusual, that in our family, poor, lacking a tradition of individual privacy and whether that is a good thing, whether all human beings should aspire to such a thing, privacy, their thoughts known only to them, to be debated and mulled over only by them, I do not know), and in all those places she found my books, the things that had come between me and the smooth flow of her life, her many children that she could not support, that she and her husband (the man not my own father) could not support, and in this fury, which she was conscious of then but cannot now remember, but which to her regret I can, she gathered all the books of mine she could find, and placing them on her stone heap (the one on which she bleached out the stains and smudges that had, in the ordinariness of life, appeared on our white clothes), she doused them with kerosene (oil from the kerosene lamp by the light of which I used to strain my eyes reading some of the books that I was about to lose) and then set fire to them. What I felt when this happened, the exact moment of the burning of my books, what I felt after this happened, the burning of my books, immediately after it happened, shortly after it happened, long after it happened, I do not know, I cannot now remember. In fact, I did not even remember that it happened at all, it had no place in the many horrible events that I could recite to friends, or the many horrible events that shaped and gave life to the thing I was to become, a writer. This event, my mother burning my books, the only thing I owned in my then-emerging life, fell into that commonplace of a cliché, the repressed memory, and there it would have remained forever if one day, while paying me a visit, while staying with me in my home, a place whose existence seemed especially miraculous—her presence only served to underline this—she had not said to a friend that if it were not for her vigilance, I would have ended up not in the home and situation that I now occupied but instead with ten children by ten different men. And she had a story to illustrate this fact: apparently, when I was about the age at which my brothers' existence—all of them—became also my responsibility (even though they were not my children, I had nothing to do with them being in the world), a boy named Lindsay used to come to our house and ask if he could borrow some of my books. This boy only pretended to love books (my mother knew this instinctively then, and she knew of this with certainty at the time she came to visit me); what she believed he wanted was to seduce me and eventually become one of the ten fathers of the ten children I would have had. One day, she said, when she grew tired of his ruse, she said to him that I had no books, that I was not a library, didn't he know. The person to whom my mother had told this story only repeated it to me when she thought my judgment of my mother had grown too harsh, had only repeated it to me to demonstrate that my mother had done the best she could and was only acting in this way to prevent me from experiencing a harsh life, to make it possible for me to have the life I had when my mother was then visiting me. I had forgotten the burning of my books, I remembered it when my friend told me the things my mother had said. And then this detail: the boy's name, Lindsay, just this boy, his name, his authentic interest in books, an interest I shared with him, and then his absence, though at the time of his sudden absence I did not note it, I did not miss it, anyway I do not remember doing so. And then so many years later, after the burning of my books and the events that led up to it, and my mother's visit in which the powerful revelation occurred, long after all this, when my brother, the one I had neglected when he was left in my charge, the one who was dying of AIDS, was hospitalized because he was almost dying before he really died, lying in the hospital room where my brother first lay when he was diagnosed with this disease, was a man named Lindsay, and when I went to visit him, this Lindsay, for I had to, no one else did, he was being treated with the same neglect and slight and fear as my brother had been by the staff of the hospital. He looked familiar, he looked like that same boy who used to come and ask me for my books, but I could not really tell if it was he or if I just wanted it to be he, so that all these events in my life would come together: my brother dying, the memory of my books being burned because I had neglected my brother who was dying when he was a small child, a boy named Lindsay who might have been one of the fathers of my numerous children, the what really happened, the what might have really happened, and how it led to what was actually happening. And then again, and then again.

This way of behaving, this way of feeling, so hysterical, so sad, when someone has died, I don't like at all and would like to avoid. It's not as if the whole thing has not happened before, it's not as if people have not been dying all along and each person left behind is the first person ever left behind in the world. What to make of it? Why can't everybody just get used to it? People are born and they just can't go on and on, and if they can't go on and on, then they must go, but it is so hard, so hard for the people left behind; it's so hard to see them go, as if it had never happened before, and so hard it could not happen to anyone else, no one but you can survive this kind of loss, seeing someone go, seeing them leave you behind; you don't want to go with them, you only don't want them to go.

On that last visit that I made to see my brother, the visit where I quarreled with him (not him with me) and I did not kiss or hug him goodbye, and even told him that I did not want to kiss or hug him and did not tell him that I loved him (and he did not say that he loved me, something he had said many times before), I spent one day trying to find Dr. Prince Ramsey. My brother was in great pain. A stream of yellow pus flowed out of his anus constantly; the inside of his mouth and all around his lips were covered with a white glistening substance, thrush. Dr. Ramsey's old office, which had been just a stone's throw from my mother's house, the house in which my brother lay dying, had been destroyed in the hurricanes (Luis, then Marilyn) and his temporary office was far away, on the All Saints Road (the road which leads to a village called All Saints) and in a building that had not been destroyed by the hurricanes, perhaps because it did not need to be, it was so dilapidated already, a building called the Hotel Bougainvillea. He was not at his office but he was expected back quite soon and I joined a group of people sitting in chairs waiting and waiting for the doctor, and we waited not in joy, not in anger, but more as if we were in a state of contemplation, as if we were seeing the whole panorama of life, from its ancient beginnings in the past to its inevitable end in some future, and we accepted it with indifference, for what else could we do? And this is the way people wait, people all over the world wait in this way, when they are powerless or poor, or both at the same time. And after I had waited for a while, his nurse, a woman who had always been so nice to me and kind to my brother, always putting me through immediately to Dr. Ramsey whenever I called, always asking after my brother and showing him sympathy, but a woman whose name I could not ever remember, told me that I most likely would find him at a funeral at two o'clock that afternoon, a funeral for a boy who was four years old.

The funeral—that is, the church part of the funeral—was being held at the Methodist church;

I knew this church well, I had been baptized in it, though this would have taken place on a weekday, not on a Sunday, because my mother and father were not married at the time I was conceived, my mother and father were never married at all; from about the time my mother was seven months pregnant with me, she and my father quarreled and they never spoke again, except in court, except when I was a grown-up woman and he complained to her about something I had written, which he had not read because he could not read, and she said some words to him, she cursed him, and so I had no parents, I had only a mother and a father, and they were not ever married, and so I could not have been baptized at the Methodist church on a Sunday, only on a weekday, though a service for my burial could have been held any day of the week. And it was in this church that I was received; that is, I became eligible to partake of Holy Communion, and I remember this passage of my life as being filled with fear, and I remember feeling already disappointed and already defeated, already hopeless, thinking and feeling that I was standing on a fragile edge and at any moment I might fall off into a narrow black hole that would amount to my entire earthly existence: I felt I hated my mother, and even worse, I felt she hated me, too; my brother Devon, the one dying just then at that moment, was one year old and I did not wish him dead; I only wished that he had never been born, because it was his birth that plunged our family into financial despair, his birth and his father's illness; and then, just around that time, his father and his and my mother, who were married, no longer liked each other ("in love" is not something I can imagine about my mother and so, too, "out of love") but did not do anything about it, for he (the father) was too old and she (my mother) is at her most intelligent when she is in a fret. Her life is a long fret.

And in that church then, the Methodist church of St. John's, Antigua (where I had been baptized and received, and where my brother who was then dying was baptized as a child, though not received, for by the time he was fourteen years of age our father, Mr. Drew—his real father, a father not really mine—was sick and took up most of our mother's attention and so he was beyond our mother's influence), there was a funeral for a four-year-old boy I did not know, and I was looking for the doctor who might keep the funeral for a man I did know at bay.

Dr. Ramsey was not in that church full of people; his wife was there, a beautiful woman I thought her so, but he, Dr. Ramsey, was not there, he was at the hospital, or visiting someone at home, or just anywhere, but he was not at the church. The church was full; in the front pews were the dead boy's immediate family and their relatives, and also his little schoolmates. The little schoolmates looked nervous and miserable (though I might have only imagined this, perhaps if I had asked them they would have said they were not miserable to be at a classmate's funeral, they were feeling something else, not miserable) and for a good reason, for they would eventually sing a hymn about the love Jesus had for little children in particular. This little boy had been dead for two weeks, but the funeral was postponed until the many relatives could come from all the corners of the earth where they had purposely and gratefully scattered themselves, for the island on which they were born could not sustain them; it could sustain other people, people born of Europe especially, but it could not sustain them, this boy's relatives; the irony of all this is that the little boy was not of Antigua, he was of the

United States; his parents had adopted him, they had the means to do so, to adopt someone from far away; someone from nearby would have only confirmed their ordinariness. But this little boy from far away, now dead and only going the way of people from near or far, the way of eternity, was in a coffin that was standing just inside the door of the church. This coffin was meant to look like a box in which precious jewels were placed: it was covered with white velvet, but instead it looked cheap, like the living-room furniture of poor people in rich countries. His immediate female relatives were all dressed in clothes made from the same cloth—a white silk with some image from the vegetable kingdom woven into it, not the animal kingdom—though not all in the same style; the men were in suits, the kinds of suits that men everywhere wear when it is said of them that they are in a suit. And this scene in my old church, the schoolchildren standing only a few feet away from their former little friend now mysteriously (for so it would have seemed to me if I had been one of them) vanished, though also surely only inside that beautiful (if you were a child) velvet box; the parents and their relatives mourning, sad, even though they were dressed so elegantly, so carefully, beautifully really, the surface of their clothing so at odds with the actual event, a funeral; the church with its big open windows, its big open doors, built many years ago by the ancestors of the people inside it, or certainly built by the ancestors of people who looked like the people now inside it; Dr. Ramsey's wife, whose son had been a classmate of the dead boy; the people just outside the church who were only passing by and who had no real interest in the events inside the church but only perhaps wanting to witness immediately, not through some remote medium, someone less fortunate (the dead boy, his parents, the people related to them), someone suffering right now: the dead, or those related to someone unfortunate enough to have died—all this made me not sad then, only now when I think of it am I sad, at the time when I was taking in the whole spectacle, at some moments I felt disdain, at some moments I felt triumphant, at some moments I felt awe, at some moments I felt bewilderment, at some moments I had a revelation; but never did I feel sad then. At the cemetery where the little boy was buried I felt curious, I wanted to get a good look at the face of the boy's mother, for at the sight of her son in his coffin being lowered into the ground, she threw up a thick colorless liquid and the other relatives and mourners did not look at her, for though there was nothing at all unusual about a mother collapsing at the sight of her own son vanishing forever from her sight, this mother's behavior did not go with her dress. Her dress was so white and pristine and proper and clean, not the thing to wear if you are going to have the dry heaves—her stomach had been emptied of even the thick, colorless liquid. And the mourners did not look at her, not only because it would have been impolite to do so, but also because the people in the place I am from do not like a vivid expression of feeling, they like only the gesture of a vivid expression of feeling, and then after the gesture they like to go home and speak of something else in which *truups*, that placing of the lips together and forcing air out through them, is heard quite frequently. And now to make that sound, the *truups*, makes my stomach feel strange, as if I am in a vessel sailing on waters I have never sailed on before, and the current is unfamiliar, and I will throw up, only I will throw up nothing solid, just a thin colorless liquid.

My friend Bud (of Bud and Connie, Bud and Connie Rabinowitz) said to me he found it strange the way people in Antigua regard illness, that when a person is ill no one mentions it, no one pays a visit; but if the person should die, there is a big outpouring of people at the funeral, there are bouquets, people sing hymns for the dead with much feeling. There was a man named Freeston (and he really *was* but *is not* anymore), and he was and is, as far as I know, the only person to publicly admit he was afflicted with the HIV virus; in making his situation public, he hoped to perform a public service. He spoke on the radio, he appeared on television, he gave talks before groups of schoolchildren. It is perhaps because of the reaction to his publicly identifying himself as a person with AIDS that no one in Antigua will do this again. The doctor who had been his permanent physician refused to see him after Freeston told him of his condition; ordinary people thought him foolish ("'E mek pappy-show of 'eself"); one day when I was visiting him and we were sitting on the gallery of his mother's house, a group of older schoolboys passed by and they called him an auntie-man and in other ways referred to his homosexuality, using vicious language; they were a chorus of intimidation, of scorn, of ignorance. Freeston was too ill to be upset, he was also quite used to it ("Me no pay dem no mine"). His mother came from that generation of Antiguan women (older, around my mother's age or older) who did not know of homosexuality, or any kind of sexuality. To say that he was gay or homosexual was something he said about himself; to say that he was an auntie-man was something people said about him. She understood him better when he was the person people said something about, not when he was the person who said something about himself. But whatever people said about him, whatever he said about himself, it did not matter to his mother; she took care of him, he lived with her in a house with a beautiful garden full of zinnias and cosmos and some impatiens and all sorts of shrubs with glossy and variegated leaves. She was so different from my brother's mother (my mother); she seemed unjudging, accepting, almost without thought (but that isn't possible); my brother's mother (my mother) was the exact opposite of all those things, and that was the thing: my brother's mother (my mother) only judged, never was accepting, had many thoughts; she was (is, for she still is) intelligent, her intelligence is like a weapon, and it has destroyed her, it destroyed some of her children: her son, my brother, was then dying. Freeston died. He went to Miami to be treated, he went to London to be treated, from London he came off the airplane in a wheelchair, and then he went to his mother's house, where he died. I do not know any details of his death; his death was not notorious, only his way to his death was so.

And my brother died, for he kept dying; each time I remembered that he had died it was as if he had just at that moment died, and the whole experience of it would begin again; my brother had died, and I didn't love him; or, at any rate, I didn't love him in the way that I had come to understand love, something so immediate it was always in front of me even when my back was turned away from it, something so immediate it was like breath itself. My children were like that, breath itself; their father was like that, breath itself; but my brother was not like that, I could breathe easily (and did breathe easily) without him in front of me, he grew up without my seeing him do so (I saw him when he was three years old and didn't see him again until he was twenty-one). I love the people I am from and I do not love the people I am from, and I do not really know what it means to say so, only that such a thing as no love now and much love now, these feelings are not permanent, or possibly not permanent. One day something may happen and I will understand that all the things I now feel, which do not at all seem like love (the word I would use to describe my feelings about my family, the people I have made my own: my husband, my children, my friends, though that word "friend" is so thin to explain that thickness), are in fact love; that I loved my brother and the other people I am from, my mother, my other brothers, and Mr. Drew (the father of my brothers, who was a father to me, though at the same time not my father at all).

His mouth so white, abloom with thrush; his lips so red, glowing, shiny from fever; his skin blackened as if his normal quotient of pigment (normal in a way unique to him, he was descended from

Africans mostly) had increased from some frightening source: his face was like a mask, and this was while he was still alive, or still amounted to something called being alive; I mean he breathed and he spoke and he took in nourishment, and fluids of different textures would pass out of his anus, and these fluids did not have a fragrance, they had a smell, and only someone trained to ignore it (a nurse, a doctor) or someone who knew him deeply (his mother) could tolerate it, or not mind it, or say "But what to do" (his mother again) in that way of total resignation and acceptance that always defeats any attempt to make something of it, to interpret it, to give it a meaning embossed, or embellished, or spare, or even neutral. His smells only made his mother (my mother) say, "But what to do." And saying that, she changed his bed, his diapers, his clothing, but could not help keeping the same tone of annoyance at the trouble he put her through and the trouble he had put her through from the beginning, when she had hoped he would not be born, and then he was, and our family could not support his added presence, and our father got sick, and I was sent away to help a family disaster that I did not create, and I did not love him because I did not know him, and then I knew him again, but then he was dying and so "What to do?" which by that time perhaps everyone in my family (that family I could not help having) said as almost a constant refrain, "What to do," and we did some things, but none of them prevented him from dying, and the moment when he realized that "What to do" would not prevent that (his dying) is a moment so universal, so common; how I wish he could have just told me: "What to do, what to do?"

And after he had died, the whiteness of his mouth, the redness of his lips, the unusual blackness of his skin, his very suffering itself began to seem sometimes as if I had made them up, though not his death itself, for everyone could remember it readily and would refer to it readily ("I'm so sorry about your brother"), and my mother was sorry about his absence ("Me miss he, you know, me miss he").

Not really more than a week after he was buried in the warm and yellow clay of the graveyard in Antigua, I resumed the life that his death had interrupted, the life with my own family, and the life of having written a book and persuading people to simply go out and buy it. I was in Chicago, a place for which I have only random memories: when I was nineteen, four girls were in my charge (I was a servant in this family) and I spent a summer looking after them in a place not far from Chicago, and I had a boyfriend whose name was Ed and he and I went to see someone famous play a guitar and sing a song in Chicago; my daughter and I once went by train to visit her father's relatives in Chicago, and while there we went to the planetarium and saw an extraordinary film about the forming of the universe, and after that we could not find a taxi to take us to the train station (the reason being no taxis appeared; the patrons of the planetarium seemed to have arrived in their own cars) and I became so afraid that we would miss our overnight train to Albany, New York, that I burst into tears, and my daughter, seeing me cry, started to cry, too, but then all of a sudden a taxi appeared and we got to the train on time and had dinner on the train and slept all through the night and then had breakfast in the morning on the train and got off and came home safely, and I want to go to Chicago on a train again but only when I am young; it is far too late for that now; and in Chicago again,

I change airplanes as I go from the Eastern part of the United States to the West. This is how Chicago used to appear in my mind when I would think of it, but that changed after my brother died.

I was in Chicago and it was so cold I should have been complaining, but I was so cheerful and agreeable that even when a man, just before he sat me down in front of him to ask me questions about the book I had written, hugged me and pressed my chest into his and ran his hands down my spine to my bottom and then up again, I did not object, I only noted it and wondered about the ups and downs of his life and what he had been like as a boy and what he had been like as a man, before he became this old man running his hands up and down my spine and bottom in a room with a few people and many bright lights; and I sat and talked to him, and then I went off and sat and talked to other people, men and women, some of them to their face, some of them through telephones, and I never told them that my brother had just died, that I was in a state of pain, a state of pain I had no real words for, a state of pain I did not know how to explain; such a thing had never happened to me before, this loss happens to other people all the time, their hair turns gray from it, loses all its natural, beautiful pigmentation: brown, black, yellow, or some combination of these, and they become gray, the color of things dying, or certainly the color of things that will know dying. But I had never been like that until my brother died; in spite of all the people I had been close to who had died, I never believed in it, the very fact that they had died; I now know that I thought of them as being somewhere else, someplace that I now no longer visited, or had never visited and would never visit, for they were there and I was here and had chosen to be here and not to join them at all; they had not died, they were only someplace else. And this made sense, for much of my life had been spent away from people who meant much to me and who were among the first people to make sense to me; I once did not see my mother for twenty years, even though I thought of her first thing in the morning and last thing at night, and almost all my thoughts of her were full of intense hatred, but she was alive and not in my sight and I could so well remember her hatred toward me—I will not add a qualifier to that, her hatred toward me, or modify it, this was just so: my mother hates her children. But that my mother might become dead, I had never imagined this.

Chicago again: how cold it was that time, so cold that I could see the lake, Lake Michigan, from my bed in the room of my extremely nice hotel, my bed so comfortable and made up twice a day, once in the morning and then again in the early evening when I was out having my dinner or talking to some of all those people in person or by telephone, and the lake was frozen, all the water in it tightly squeezed together, all bound up into ice, and the ice was blue, not an inviting blue, like the sky sometimes, or the sea sometimes, but a blue that is the color of a dress that might cost so much only two or three people in the world can afford to buy it, or like a blue of something that is far away in another part of the universe, such a blue was the frozen water in the lake that time; and it was so cold everybody talked about it. It's so cold, they said, at first as if it were a surprise and then as if it were a punishment: "It's so cold!" It was cold, just the opposite of the earth and the atmosphere where my brother had just been buried, and this cold allowed me to think of him without mentioning him to anyone or telling them of my predicament, that at the moment I seemed to be having such a triumph, a book I had written interested people who knew nothing at all about me (for is that not a desire of people who on writing books allow them to be published and exposed to a public: that people who do not know them, absolute strangers, will buy the book and read it and then like it). They did not know that I had suffered a great loss: someone I did not know I loved had died, someone I did not want to love had died, and that dying had a closed-door quality to it, a falling-off-the-horizon quality to it, the end, an end, nothing . . . and yet, what to do? For it is the end and yet so many things linger.

But. I was reading from the book I had written to an audience in a bookstore (and my reading was not complicated by my feelings of sympathy for the owner of this small bookstore, who had her own worries about the ruthlessness of capitalism and the ruthlessness of the marketplace—the two things synonymous and making her ability to earn a living in the way she chose difficult—and the ruthlessness of life itself, and though she never did say this, I gathered, I felt, she meant her own worthiness made her exempt from all this, marketplace, capitalism, life itself; I was sympathetic, since I feel exactly that way about my own self), and the audience was very kind and I was grateful that there were so many people, for it was so cold, and I saw some of my husband's relatives in the audience and that made me happy, for it is so easy to love people you do not really know and only have the strong feeling that you should love them because they perhaps remind you of the people you love best in the world, the people you have chosen, and so I was happy, in a way, or almost happy, in a way. And then, just as the room was emptying out, I saw a face that I recognized from somewhere else. I didn't know where, except I knew it wasn't a dream I had had, or someone who was a part of my intimate life in the past (my intimate past being my youth, which was full of curiosity and conviction and courage, and since I have survived it, my intimate past, I simply shall never repeat it); it was just the face of a woman with thin skin (it was empty of pigment and so thin in color) and short hair, like a boy who has been bad and a part of his punishment is to have his head shorn of hair: a humiliation. And to this face I said, "Hello," tentatively, unsure, for so many times I have greeted a familiar face with enthusiasm only to have the person say they don't know me at all and have never seen me before, and I never get the impression that they want to know me more or see me again. And so I said, "Hello," and this person said, "Hello," and when I said that she looked familiar, she told me that yes, we had been in an AIDS support group in Antigua three years before. I said, Oh yes, and I remembered that whole afternoon of the AIDS support group listening to Dr. Ramsey and viewing his display of slides depicting all sorts of stages of sexually transmitted diseases with the sexual organs looking so decayed the viewer could almost smell the decay just by looking at them. And I remembered this woman, superior and slightly contemptuous of her general surroundings (but I did not fault her for that, I had felt the same way, only more so) and casting blame and making denunciations (and I did not fault her for that, I had futilely gone so far as to write a small book in which I did nothing but cast blame and make denunciations), and just in general making everyone present at the meeting wish a little that she was not there, not at the meeting but somewhere in the world where she would do good beyond imagining, but at this meeting, who was she? She was far more disturbing than the woman with thick skin who had opinions about the evil of white people and the goodness of black people—her words—and though I shall never be surprised by the aversion human beings can feel toward each other, for even I found her ways of arriving at her opinions offensive (but that is only a polite way of my now saying that at the time she said these things, if there had been an acceptable rubbish heap for human beings who said rubbishy things, I would have placed her on it. But how would I have achieved such an ability?). All these thoughts overwhelmed me, though they did not cripple me, but I was overwhelmed all the same, trying to place her in those new moments when I had just discovered that my brother was dying, would die, and that I did not love him, or did not recognize my feelings for him as being love, but felt such a responsibility, an obligation, to help him in some way. And just seeing her face made me say the thing I had not been saying at all, only thinking as a separate person, not the person in the room reading; I had been thinking, My brother has just died, my brother has died, but to her I said, as simply as this, "My brother died," and she said as simply as this, "I know."

When she said this, "I know," a whole world

rolled out in front of me, not falling off a desk and crashing like the miniature water-filled glass domes which my children collect and always ask me to be on the lookout for when I go somewhere new, and these water-filled domes, with a little make-believe scene stuck to their bottom, a scene with a symbol of some city or figure associated with the pleasures of childhood, are always falling off my children's desks or dressers, just falling from a high place and crashing, and water and scene of city or scene associated with childhood pleasures scatter all over the floor, and then all of it soon becomes invisible to the naked eye, but the bare sole of a foot feels its invisible remains and the shattered dome then registers as something dangerous and sinister because it can be felt but never seen. And so it was not like a shattered miniature water-filled dome with a scene of any kind that this woman whose face I had seen before, whose voice I had heard before but now in Chicago was saying "I know," seemed to me; it was not like that at all; it was like something unrolling, a carpet, a sheet of paper, and I knew it would hold a surprise, but this did not frighten me, I was indifferent to fear right then, but only right then; ordinarily I am not indifferent to fear at all; ordinarily I am quite afraid of the consequences of the thing I am about to do, but I do it anyway. But that "I know." Her voice surely would have been sympathetic, she must have lowered her head, I always lower my head when I feel sympathy or something tender for people who need sympathy. She only said, "I know." And I said, "How did you know?" and I said, "Did you know my brother?" And she said yes. And then she said that she had been a lesbian woman living in Antigua and how deeply sad it made her to see the scorn and derision heaped on the homosexual man; homosexual men had no place to go in Antigua, she said, no place to simply meet and be with each other and not be afraid; and so she had opened up her home and made it known that every Sunday men who loved other men could come to her house in the afternoon and enjoy each other's company. My brother, she said, was a frequent visitor to her house. She only said all that. On Sundays men who were homosexuals came to her house, a safe place to be with each other, and my brother who had just died was often at her house, not as a spectator of homosexual life but as a participant in homosexual life.

A great sadness overcame me, and the source of the sadness was the deep feeling I had always had about him: that he had died without ever understanding or knowing, or being able to let the world in which he lived know, who he was; that who he really was—not a single sense of identity but all the complexities of who he was—he could not express fully: his fear of being laughed at, his fear of meeting with the scorn of the people he knew best were overwhelming and he could not live with all of it openly. His homosexuality is one thing, and my becoming a writer is another altogether, but this truth is not lost to me: I could not have become a writer while living among the people I knew best, I could not have become myself while living among the people I knew best—and I only knew them best because I was from them, of them, and so often felt I was them—and they were—are—the people who ought to have loved me best in the whole world, the people who should have made me feel that the love of people other than them was suspect. And his life unfolded before me not like a map just found, or a piece of old paper just found, his life unfolded and there was everything to see and there was nothing to see; in his life there had been no flowering, his life was the opposite of that, a flowering, his life was like the bud that sets but, instead of opening into a flower, turns brown and falls off at your feet.

And in the unfolding were many things, all contained in memory (but without memory what would be left? Nothing? I do not know): the girl from Guiana with whom he had been having unprotected sex after he knew he was infected with the HIV virus; the girl (another one altogether) who saw him sunning himself on the veranda of the hospital that first time when he had been seriously ill and the doctors thought he would be dead in three days—she had known him very well, she had been used to being seduced by him in one way or another, but when she saw him so thin in the hospital, so weak, my brother could tell that she had heard the rumors about him (they were true, but he could not admit it to himself then, and she was not really sure), and the way she distanced herself from him caused him great pain (he was dying and should have been beyond that, but dying was very new to him then); and the flirting with the nurses in Dr. Ramsey's office who knew of his situation, and he knew that they knew of his situation, and so their scorn (they did not hide it) must have been especially painful, but I did not know, he could not (I now see) let me know; and then again their scorn was painful to him because in it his secret of not really wanting to seduce them, really wanting to seduce someone who was not at all like them, a man, became clear to him, was made plain to him, and so the doubleness of his life, which was something he could manage ordinarily, in a day-in, day-out situation, must have been erased in those moments, and perhaps he despaired that the walls separating the parts of his life had broken down, and that might have caused him much anxiety, and such a thing, the anxiety when it appeared on his face, would have seemed to me, who knew nothing about his internal reality, as another kind of suffering, a suffering I might be able to relieve with medicine I had brought from the prosperous North; but I did not know then, I only know now. And in this Now, I can understand why a man, a teacher, though not an old teacher, would want to take him on a journey to Trinidad, just the two of them together, and my brother not being able to pay his own way was no hindrance to this plan; but this whole incident of the teacher—a man—who wanted to take him on a trip, a holiday, the why of it, is clear to me now, the why part of it; I only asked this question at the time he was dying, and again after he was dead.

And then again, when thinking of that woman in the bookstore in Chicago, her white hair cropped short and lying close to her scalp (though not in a forced way, it lay on her head quite naturally), the way she emerged from the damp and blue cold and the dark night, with her tale of regular secret meetings on Sunday afternoons in a climate the direct opposite of the one we were in, I, even I, with all my New World sophistication (this New World in which I now live began in 1492 and for very convenient reasons it insists on this status, "New World," people from everywhere else, for myriad reasons, need it to be a "New World"), wondered, and then doubted, and went back and forth, whether she was telling me something true or just something she wished to say: Your brother came to my house because my house offered him a setting to be himself, his real self, a self which loved the deep intimacy and companionship of other men, a self of which he was ashamed and afraid to show to anyone other than the people who were sympathetic to and shared his secret. And I returned to my room in the hotel, a room from which I could see the water of Lake Michigan stilled, frozen, blue in color, but the frozen waters of Lake Michigan were a blue not like a blue my brother had ever seen, it was not like the blue of the Atlantic Ocean in the West Indies (the Atlantic Ocean in Nova Scotia or Martha's Vineyard is not blue at all, it is a gray, a gray that signals the beginning of the end of things); nor was it like the blue of the Caribbean Sea, another body of water my brother might have been familiar with; oh, but he was familiar with it, I have seen him swimming in it, and later when he was dying he gave me his school textbook, *A History of the West Indies.* No, it was a captive blue, this blue of Lake Michigan, a blue that held in it restraint and at the same time destruction; it was not permanent, this frozen water and color of the lake which I could see from my hotel, and each room of this hotel cost a great deal of money, money that my brother might have wanted and even imagined, but by that time he was dead, I had buried him a week or so ago, and I could only go back to that room that cost so much and imagine my brother, his life, and my own, which was in direct contrast to his. I was alive, I was in danger of not being so only in the usual way, the airplane on which I flew from place to place might fall out of the sky, a vessel in my brain might suddenly burst, my heart might be stilled as if someone had reached in and stopped it, like a clock on a wall, like the mechanical toy my son winds up and makes go and then, for a reason that pleases solely him, places in the palm of his hand, squeezing all its mechanism until it just stops; my life could end in the manner of all those things. Just then it had not, just yet, just now, at this moment that I am sitting and contemplating (though I am not sure that I am capable of contemplation), I am remembering the life of my brother, I am remembering my own life, or at least a part of my own life, for my own life is still ongoing, I hope, and each moment of its present shapes its past and each moment of its present will shape its future and even so influence the way I see its future; and the knowledge of all this leaves me with the feeling: And what now, and so, yes, what now. *What now!*

But the feeling that his life with its metaphor of the bud of a flower firmly set, blooming, and then the blossom fading, the flower setting a seed which bore inside another set of buds, leading to flowers, and so on and so on into eternity—this feeling that his life actually should have provided such a metaphor, so ordinary an image, so common and so welcoming had it been just so, could not leave me; and I was haunted by everything that had happened since he died and everything that had happened before he died, and everything that was happening as I went from the city of Chicago and its view of the frozen lake of blue, a blue that was not permanent, a blue that would change with the season (a thing my brother would never know, a change of season, for he never left the place in which he was born).

Once, when I was looking for a new dress to wear to a ceremony during which my husband would receive an award, I bought a white dress with blue stripes, a dress I liked (though it was not the dress I finally wore to the ceremony, I later bought a plain white dress and wore that to the ceremony) because it reminded me of a dress worn by children (though it was a dress my own daughter, ten at the time, would never wear, too childish, she would say), and perhaps I bought it because I was just becoming old enough (I was forty-six) to want innocence again and old enough to convince any observer that the appearance of innocence at my age was meant to be my actual innocence at the age when I was actually innocent. I bought this dress; it had an Empire waistline, it had gathers under the breast, the length of the skirt came to just above my ankles. It was this dress I wore to my brother's funeral. I bought it at the moment I was thinking of celebrating the honor my husband had been given, but it was that dress I wore to my brother's funeral; and at the time I wore it to his funeral I thought to myself, I will never wear this dress again, I can never wear this dress again, and as I write this, it is true: I have never worn that dress again. I tried to give it away, but the person to whom I tried to give the dress was too old for it, she was sixty-one years old and was too short for it, the skirt dragged on the floor, and she was too stout for it, the zipper in the back would not go above the point that was her waist. And the airplane I flew on to his burial was blue, and the sky in which the airplane flew was blue, and there was the white of the clouds; and the water surrounding the land, the ground in which he was buried, that water was blue, and that water, the water surrounding the land in which he was buried, was sometimes flecked with white, the foam caused by the rush of the waves as they dashed against the shore. But the color blue did not run through all my memories, or all my experiences; on the whole, every scene, every memory remained itself, just itself, and sometimes a certain color might make memory more vivid and sometimes again, not so at all, just not so at all; sometimes a memory is without color, a dream is often like that, without color, but the absence of color does not mean an absence of truth, or truth in a way that one could understand as not a falsehood. Oh, how I wished never to think about him again, never to see blue and say, "What did Devon think of that, such a color," or think, Here is the sound of something that reminded me of Devon, or something that if Devon had heard of, he would have been propelled into a world in which he could delay his death, or just simply taunt its inevitability, for his death was inevitable, as was mine (as is mine, but at that time in his life my own death would have been an accident or a surprise, not something anyone expected).

And then he died, not in the middle of the night, which was the hour he was born, but in the very early morning, at about five o'clock, the hour I was born; and I know the hour he was born because I was there, and I know the hour I was born and the hour he died because our mother has told me. And all that night as he was dying, he called out over and over again the names of his brothers, and he called out for his mother. He called her "Muds" then, short for Mother, but when he was well and when he was young, he called her Mrs. Drew, which is her married name; when he was well and when he was young he did not like to show any dependence on her and so he called her what any ordinary person would call her, but perhaps it was only to disguise how much he needed her, for he never ever made a home for himself apart from his mother. He called out for his brothers; he called out, "Dalma": Dalma was the brother he was closest to and they had played cricket together when they were small boys, and they were together when Mr. Drew, their father, our mother's husband, died in the hospital all alone one night after he had suffered a stroke; they were in the house together at the very moment Mr. Drew had suffered the stroke.

It was Dalma who gave him, Devon, the name "Patches," because he liked to place patches of different-colored cloth all over his clothes regardless of their needing such a thing as a patch. And Dalma would call him by that name when he—Dalma—came home from one of his three jobs ("Hey, Patches, how you doing, mahn, how you doing?"), and people who knew him from when he was a boy, a student at Boys School, would call him that, "Patches." And when he was dying he called Dalma, he said, "Dalma," the only name he had ever called that brother. His other brother's name was Joseph, and he was generally called Joe, only Devon called him "Styles," because when they were boys Devon had noticed that Joe was very particular about the way he looked and would always dress in a way that might be called stylish, and so Joe was known to him as "Styles," and I do not know if Joe ever liked being called that, for those two brothers did not get along, and when Devon first learned that he was dying it vexed him so to see Joe in good health, it vexed him so to think that Joe would continue to live after he had died and inherit his little house, the coffinlike structure their mother had built for him, or any other thing that was his ("Me bex, you know, me bex, me no want he get me tings"). And yet "Styles" is the last thing he said, only that, "Styles," and then there was silence, a silence so ordinary that my mother thought he had fallen asleep at last, exhausted from calling out the names of his mother and his brother that he was close to ("loved" must be the word) and the brother that he did not like so much, the brother he could not bear to have inherit the little house he used to live in. When the silence fell, how relieved my mother was then, she told me so later, and when telling me so, she was full of sorrow, and I had sympathy for her then, but still no love, only sympathy, and some revulsion, as if I felt what had just happened to her—her child had died, she would be burying one of her children—was a contagious disease and just to be around her, just to be so near her meant I might catch it, this thing of burying your children when they are still so young, when they have not really lived at all.

And that night he was dying in the dark of that small room, thirty-three years of age, with none of the traditional attachments ordinary to a man his age—thirty-three—a wife, a companion of some kind, children, his own house, even a house he rented, his own bed (I had gone to a furniture store one day and purchased the one which he lay dying on, and even as I did that, I could remember his father, Mr. Drew, repairing the crib that he lay in when he was a baby just born, but that crib was first made for Joe and then refurbished for Dalma and then refurbished again for his birth; I don't remember that too much attention was lavished on the crib by the time he arrived, because his arrival pushed the family to a brink over which we all fell, our family was never the same after his birth).

He had read in a novel written by me about a mother who had tried and tried and failed and failed to abort the third and last of her three male children. And when he was dying he asked me if that mother was his mother and if that child was himself ("Ah me de trow'way pickney"); in reply, I laughed a great big Ha! Ha! and then said no, the book he read is a novel, a novel is a work of fiction; he did not tell me that he did not believe my reply and I did not tell him that he should not believe my reply.

That night as he lay dying and calling the names of his brothers and his mother, he did not call my name, and I was neither glad nor sad about this. For why should he call my name? I knew him for the first three years of his life, I came to know him again in the last three years of his life, and in the time between I had changed my name, I did not have the name our mother had given to me, and though he always called me by the new name I had given myself, he did not know the self I had become (which isn't to say that I know this, the self I have become), he did not know who I was, and I can see that in the effort of dying, to make sense of me and all that had happened to me between the years he was three and thirty was not only beyond him but also of no particular interest to him. And that feeling of his lack of interest in me, his sister, not being included in the roll call of his family, seemingly forgotten by him in the long hours before he left the world, seems so natural, so perfect; he was so right! I had never been a part of the tapestry, so to speak, of Patches, Styles, and Muds; I had only heard about the time he was involved in murdering a gas-station attendant and our mother used her substantial political connections to get him out of jail, his sentence reduced because he became a witness against the others, his friends, who along with him were involved in this murder, and then his emerging to live a life made up of strong feelings (positive feelings) for a man who was king of a small country in a landlocked part of Africa (Haile Selassie of Ethiopia), smoking the leaves of a plant which would cause him to have hallucinations. I shall never forget him, my brother, but this was not because of his smile, or the way he crossed a swelling river and saved a dog, or his sense of humor, or his love of John Milton (he loved not so much John Milton as all the people who came after and were influenced by John Milton; but all the people he met who came after John Milton and were influenced by John Milton were servants in the British colonial enterprise); I shall never forget him because his life is the one I did not have, the life that, for reasons I hope shall never be too clear to me, I avoided or escaped. Not his fate, for I, too, shall die, only his life, with its shadows dominating the brightness, its shadows eventually overtaking its brightness, so that in the end anyone wanting to know him would have to rely on that, shadows; and in the shadows of his life is a woman emerging from an audience in a bookstore in Chicago and telling me of secrets in his life, his life as he lived it in the shadows.

And at the time he was dying, all through that night, all through the night I was a continent away, seated in an airplane as it flew through the dark atmosphere, then sitting in the falsely lighted rooms in the airport, waiting for planes to transport me home to my family, traveling through these spaces in a natural dark and then a false light, carrying plants (those rhododendrons, native to a part of the world, New Guinea, that was foreign to me but has shaped my memory all the same: plants that would make prosper a population of annoying small flies in my house and then die, and nothing I could do, no remedy in any of many plant encyclopedias I have, could save them. They bloomed beautifully and then died, dying, as always, being so irreversible).

My mother's house after he was dead was empty of his smell, but I did not know that his dying had a smell until he was dead and no longer in the house, he was at the undertaker's, and I never asked my mother about the smells in the house. I wanted to see what he looked like when he was dead and so I had asked the undertaker not to do anything to his body before I arrived. Only now, a little more than a year later, I wonder how I knew to say such a thing, for I am grateful (only because I would have wondered, been haunted about it, and so now my interest is satisfied, even as it raises another kind of interest, another haunting) that I did, but at the time it happened—he was dead, I had been told so—I felt removed from events, I wished something else was happening, I wished I was complaining about some luxury that was momentarily causing me disappointment: the lawn mower wouldn't work, my delicious meal in a restaurant was not at an ideal temperature, a meadow I loved to walk past never achieved a certain beauty that I wanted it to achieve.

He was in a plastic bag with a zipper running the length of its front and middle, a plastic bag of good quality, a plastic bag like the ones given to customers when they buy an expensive suit at a store that carries expensive clothing. The zipper coming undone sounded just like a zipper coming undone, like a dangerous reptile warning you of its presence; oh, but then again, it was so much like the sound of a zipper, just any zipper, or this particular zipper, the zipper of the bag which held my brother's body (for he was that, my brother's body). He looked as if he had been deliberately drained of all fluids, as if his flesh had been liquefied and that, too, drained out. He did not look like my brother, he did not look like the body of my brother, but that was what he was all the same, my brother who had died, and all that remained of him was lying in a plastic bag of good quality. His hair was uncombed, his face was unshaven, his eyes were wide-open, and his mouth was wide-open, too, and the open eyes and the open mouth made it seem as if he was looking at something in the far distance, something horrifying coming toward him, and that he was screaming, the sound of the scream silent now (but it had never been heard, I would have been told so, it had never been heard, this scream), and this scream seemed to have no break in it, no pause for an intake of breath; this scream only came out in one exhalation, trailing off into eternity, or just trailing off to somewhere I do not know, or just trailing off into nothing.

My husband's father had died four years before, and when I had seen him dead, I had a strong desire to tell him what it was like when he died, all the things that happened, what people said, what they did, how they behaved, how his death made them feel; he would not have liked hearing about it at all, I knew that, but I also knew how curious he was about experiences he did not like or want to have, and that one of the ways I became a writer was by telling my husband's father things he didn't want me to tell him but was so curious about that he would listen to them anyway.

My brother would not have wanted to hear how he looked when he died, he would not have wanted to know how everyone behaved, what they said and what they did. He would not have wanted to know anything about it, except if someone had a mishap; an embarrassing mishap would have made him laugh, he loved to laugh at other people's mishaps, I cannot remember him showing sympathy, and yet I do not remember him being cruel, his own mother was cruel. He would have found his death —his lying in the plastic bag of good quality, his mouth open, his eyes staring into something, a void that might hold all of meaning, or staring into nothing in particular—funny, but only if it was happening to someone else. I do not know, I do not know. And when next I saw him again, lying in the coffin made of pitch pine, the wood which Mr. Drew, his father, my mother's husband, a carpenter, used mainly to make all sorts of furniture, his hair was nicely combed and dyed black—for how else could it have gotten to such a color—his lips were clamped tightly together and they made a shape that did not amount to his mouth as I had known it; and his eyes had been sewn shut, sewn shut, and I have to say it again, sewn shut. And so he looked like an advertisement for the dead, not like the dead at all; for to be dead young cannot be so still, so calm, only the still alive know death to be still and calm; I only say this after having seen my brother just dead, before the people still in life arranged him. My mother said that the body in the coffin did not look like her son at all (" 'E no look like 'e, 'e no look like Devon"), and that was true, but it was only that he did not look like the Devon we had gotten used to looking at as he got sick and then declined amazingly into death, living while being dead. She forgot that for a long time he did not look like Devon, the Rastafarian, the reggae singer, the seducer of women (we did not and cannot now know what he looked like as the seducer of men), that the body in the coffin was of someone we did not know, the body lying there would never become familiar to us, it would have no likes and dislikes, it would never say anything memorable, we would never quarrel with it, he was dead. The undertaker went among the mourners asking if we wanted one last look before the coffin lid was put in place, and after that all views of him on this earth would be no more.

Such a moment, a final goodbye, must be complicated. I put it this way, "must be," because this was something happening in my life, a real thing, something so important that I wanted my own children to witness it. I had taken them with me to visit him, I had taken them with me when he died, and they, too, viewed his body before the undertaker had transformed him from someone just dead to someone ready to be seen just before his burial. And so, goodbye. My mother looked at him for the last time, his brothers looked at him for the last time, I looked at him for the last time, my children looked at him for the last time, my mother's friends from her church looked at him for the last time, some men his age who knew him from school, who had not seen him when he was sick but now attended his funeral, looked at him for the last time. Oh, the indignity to be found in death; just as well that the dead seem unable to notice it.

It was in that funeral home in which he lay that I first encountered the dead. The dead then was a girl with a hunchback and I did not know her, I only saw her on the street in her school uniform, but her deformity had made her well known to other schoolchildren who were not deformed at all, and so when she died I wanted to see what she looked like. Seeing her lying in her coffin created a sense of wonder in me; seeing my brother did not, but that might have been because by the time my brother died I was so old that the idea of death seemed possible, but still only possible, something other people might decide to do. When I had seen the girl with the hunchback lying dead in her coffin, my brother was not yet born, and even my own life, the life that I now live, was not yet born, and so I could not imagine, would not have been capable of wondering, if this place, Straffee's funeral parlor (the funeral parlor where the girl lay, the funeral parlor where my brother lay), would resonate in me, would come up in any way in my life again. My brother's body lay not in the same room as hers, he lay in the room next to the one in which her body had been; the funeral parlor had expanded, and in any case, the room in which she had lain held another body, another funeral, a man thirty-five years old who also had died of AIDS, or the virus that causes AIDS, or something like that;

whatever is the right way to say it, he had died of the same thing as my brother. Mr. Straffee, the owner of the funeral parlor, died in the same year as my brother; Mr. Straffee was very old then, and I cannot tell if he got involved in such, the business of burying people, to accustom himself to the idea of his own death, or if he hoped such an intimacy with death would protect him from its actual occurrence, or lessen his fear of its actual occurrence.

My brother's coffin was most plain, it was in the category of the ones that cost less, pitch pine stained with a very dark varnish. I had known how much it would cost, and so before I returned for his funeral I went to the bank in the small town in which I lived and purchased traveler's checks. The undertaker took payment in traveler's checks.

His funeral procession was not large, and there might have been many reasons for this. He had died of a disease that carried a powerful social stigma. People in the place that I am from are quite comfortable with the shame of sex, the inexplicable need for it, an enjoyment of it that seems beyond the ordinary, the actual peculiarity of it; only then when you die from it, sex, does the shame become, well, shame. Then he was not a well-known person, a famous person, and this would have disappointed him, he so longed to be well known and well thought of. Funerals in Antigua have always been social events, especially the funerals of young people, but he was not so young, he was not well known, he died of a disease that had a great shame attached to it.

His death, and so his funeral, was not like that of the little boy, only four years old, who died while taking a swimming lesson with his schoolmates in the seawater at Fort James, just died suddenly, fainting, losing consciousness and then dying, and that is what was said of his death: he just died suddenly, while learning to swim; he fainted and lost consciousness and then died. He lay in a refrigerator in a funeral home, the same funeral home that took care of my brother's burial, while his mother's and father's relatives who were living in various parts of the world, all far away from Antigua, in climates different from the one in Antigua, returned to Antigua. His mother and some close female relatives of both his parents all wore brand-new dresses made from the same material, though not in the same style, and also, they did not show their feelings of sorrow at the same time. The church service part of this little boy's funeral was held in the same church in which my brother (and I) had been christened and confirmed (the Methodist church, though in that tradition you are received not confirmed), and I had no real feelings when I saw that his coffin was in the same place, in front of the altar where I had taken my first communion and just plain communion many times after that. I was, at that moment I was seeing his coffin, trying to find my brother's doctor, Dr. Prince Ramsey. The church was filled with the dead four-year-old boy's relatives and their friends, people were standing on the steps of the church trying to see the little coffin and of course the family, because the sorrow expressed by the family, the sorrow shown by the family excites observers, evoking pity for the mourner and, ultimately, superiority, for to see someone suffer in a moment when you are not suffering can inspire such a feeling, superiority, in a place like Antigua, with its history of subjugation, leaving in its wake humiliation and inferiority; to see someone in straits worse than your own is to feel at first pity for them and soon better than them. And so it was that a large number of people who did not know this little boy or any member of his family but had heard of his death through hearsay had come to see his little coffin, something made out of cheap wood and then covered with white velvet, and had come to see his family suffer over their loss. His little classmates stood not far from the coffin, and later they sang a song about Jesus and his particular love for children. The children were not at the graveyard, and so they did not see his mother as she wept over his coffin being lowered into the ground and his mother weeping and throwing up nothing but mucus, the only thing left in her stomach. The children did not see this, but many onlookers did, they saw the mother vomiting nothing but mucus at the sight of her son's coffin being lowered into the ground, and the father, her husband, holding her up after she had slumped to the ground, and then leading her away from the grave to sit on a grave nearby, a grave of someone I do not believe they knew, yet it was a good place to sit all the same. I was at the graveyard still looking for Dr. Ramsey, but he was not there, and when next I saw him in the graveyard, it was at my brother's funeral, and between that boy's burial and my brother's death I saw and spoke to Dr. Ramsey many times, but on that day I did not see him.

And so my brother's funeral; the undertaker (and it was not at that moment that I first made the observation that an undertaker often looks like a corpse in one way or another: bloated like a dead body that has been neglected, or thin and emaciated like a dead body properly preserved so that it decays slowly, dryly, or like a dead body that has been carefully manicured and tended to make the relatives doubt slightly the sight they are witnessing: I am looking at the dead)—the undertaker called us, his family, to take a last look at him, and this call for a last look only reminded me of scenes in other narrative forms in which there is a bartender and just before the bar closes there is a last call for drinks. We all looked at him, I and his and my mother, my brother who no longer speaks to my mother even though they continue to live in the same house, and my other brother, who broke my mother's neck by throwing her onto the ground in the process of trying to stop her from throwing stones at him because she disapproved of him bringing a girlfriend, or any woman with whom he had a sexual relationship, into the structure where he—they all—lived; this structure was so near to my mother's own house that she could hear all their conversations and all their sounds, and the conversations and sounds were an abomination to her (and that is the word for the feelings that roiled in her heart toward his actions, his wanting to live: abomination!), and when he would not cease this behavior of which she disapproved she first quarreled with him and then threw stones at him, and while trying to stop her from stoning him (and this was not exactly a defense of himself, for I say a defense of himself would have been to throw stones back at her), he threw her to the ground and broke her neck; it was a break so serious that she should have died or become a quadriplegic, yet she recovered so completely that she has buried one of her own children. When once she was complaining to me about her health, I jokingly said, "Oh, Mother, you will bury us all"; she said in reply, "You think so," and she laughed, but I did not laugh, I could not laugh, I was—am—one of the "us." There were her two sons still alive, and then there was me, her only daughter, but not Devon's only sister in the world, for his father, Mr. Drew, had had other girl children with other mothers, but I was his only sister at his funeral, and I, too, went to take a last look at him, but it was unreal the way he looked: his hair styled in a way I had never seen it styled when I knew him alive; his eyes closed, shut, sealed, like an envelope, not a vault; his body was delicate, fragile-seeming, all bones, finally stilled, not ever so slightly moving up and down; his farawayness so complete, so final, he shall never speak again; he shall never speak again in the everyday way that I speak of speech.

The coffin lid was put in place and the sounds of the screws securing it did not cause us to cry or vomit or pass out. My mother said it did not look like Devon at all, and that was true, but I did not know which Devon she meant: Was it the baby a day old almost eaten alive by red ants, or was it the two-year-old boy who was left in my charge and whose diaper I neglected to change as it became filled with his still-baby feces because I had become absorbed in a book; or was it the Devon who was involved in the homicide of a gas-station attendant; or the one who played cricket so well and learned to swim at Country Pond; or the one who smoked the Weed, the way she referred to his marijuana addiction; or the one who changed from a vibrant young man who had come down with a very bad case of pneumonia and then was told in an open hospital ward by a doctor accompanied by two nurses that he had the HIV virus and that shortly he would be dead; or the one who was well enough shortly after that to begin having unprotected sex with women and sex with other people who were not women but who we—that is, his family—did not know about? Which Devon was he? All of them, I suppose; and which did he like best, and which one of his selves made him happiest? I cannot tell this, and perhaps neither could he.

And that day that he was buried was not at all unlike the day on which I first saw him lying almost dead in a bed in the Gweneth O'Reilly ward of the Holberton Hospital. All days in Antigua must be the same, people count on it, it is for this reason they go there, it is for this reason they leave there; the days are the same, the sun shines, no rain will fall, the sun rises at around six in the morning, the sun sets at around six in the evening; if this does not remain so, it is a catastrophe; a hurricane can change this, or the coming-awake of a volcano, but Antigua does not have such a thing as a volcano. He died on a sunny day, he was buried on a sunny day. At the funeral parlor there were people milling around outside and I did not know them, but that made sense when I realized that there was another young man being buried, a young man with a family and not many friends; he, too, had died of AIDS. His grave was not more than twenty yards away from my brother's, and their graveside ceremonies coincided; the families and friends of the two dead men did not speak to one another; the two men were buried at the margins of the cemetery, far away from the entrance, and this was so not because of the thing that had caused their death but because of something that long ago perhaps had the same social stigma as AIDS: they or their families were not members of respectable churches. The other man was buried in the place reserved for Seventh-Day Adventists, my brother was buried in the place reserved for the Church of the Nazarene. Nothing about their death ceremonies made communication between their families occur; not sharing the same funeral parlor, not sharing the margin of the burial ground. The other dead man's family did not say a sympathetic word to us and we did not say a sympathetic word to them. The Church of the Nazarene was our mother's church, she attended services there regularly, her fellow church members came often to pray with my brother, though he did not believe in anything himself, except if he thought, just at the moment he needed to, that faith in the thing in front of him might serve him well. But he died, and on the way to the church part of the service, we passed some men who were in a yard, sitting under a tree making coffins, and they looked up as we passed by, perhaps to see their handiwork, for his coffin had been made by them, they worked for Mr. Straffee, and also out of curiosity, for it must be true for them, too, even as they make these houses for the dead that are in constant demand, the wondering if it is something real, will it happen to them; if it is so certain, death, why is it such a surprise, why is everybody who is left behind, who is not dead, in a state of such shock, as if this thing, death, this losing forever of someone who means something to you, has never happened before. Why is it so new, why is this worn-out thing, death, someone dying, so new, so new?

And yet when the minister preached a sermon about us all being reunited at some later date, I did not like that at all, I wanted to tell him that I did not want to see these people with whom I had shared so much—a womb in the case of my brother, blood and breath in the case of my mother—I did not want to be with any of these people again in another world. I had had enough of them in this one; they mean everything to me and they mean nothing, and even so, I do not really know what I mean when I say this. My brother, the one who lives in the same house as my mother but who does not speak to her and will not make a reply to her no matter what she says to him, and says he would not make a reply to her even if she asked him to save her life, especially if she asked him to save her life (and he is not the one who threw her down and broke her neck, a break that should have left her dead or crippled from the waist down and instead she made a complete recovery and has buried one of her children so far), this brother said a few words about his dead sibling, the one he had named "Patches," but he did not mention that, the part about the name Patches, he only recalled that Devon loved to play cricket, how close they had been when they were schoolboys together; he did not say how afraid they were when their father (Mr. Drew) died and they did not want to attend his funeral and hid from our mother, who had to beat them (in one case) or threaten to beat them (in another case) to attend; he did not say how his dead brother's carelessness with his own life might have led to such an early death and was a contrast to his own caution and industriousness (he held three jobs: an accountant, a peddler of imported foods in the market, and a bass-steel-drum player in the most prominent steel band in Antigua). His voice broke as he spoke of his brother; I cried when I heard him speak of his brother, but why did he and I do that, for so many times we used to say that if by some miracle Devon could be cured of his disease he would not change his ways; he would not become industrious, holding three jobs at once to make ends meet; he would not become faithful to one woman or one man. But this was the end and he was lying in the coffin, the least expensive coffin in Mr. Straffee's display of coffins for adults; he was thin, so diminished that his bedclothes and bed linen, freshly cleaned by his mother, had to be packed inside the coffin to keep his body from rattling around (though really he would not have been able to hear it and he certainly would not have been able to feel it).

I became a writer out of desperation, so when I first heard my brother was dying I was familiar with the act of saving myself: I would write about him. I would write about his dying. When I was young, younger than I am now, I started to write about my own life and I came to see that this act saved my life. When I heard about my brother's illness and his dying, I knew, instinctively, that to understand it, or to make an attempt at understanding his dying, and not to die with him, I would write about it.

For many years I wrote for a man named William Shawn. Whenever I thought of something to write, I immediately thought of him reading it, and the thought of this man, William Shawn, reading something I had written only made me want to write it more; I could see him sitting (not in any particular place) and reading what I had written and telling me if he liked it, or never mentioning it again if he didn't, and the point wasn't to hear him say that he liked it (though that was better than anything in the whole world) but only to know that he had read it, and why that should have been so is beyond words to me right now, or just to put it into words now (and it was only through words that I knew him) would make it either not true, or incomplete, like love, I suppose: why do I love you, why do you love me? Almost all of my life as a writer, everything I wrote I expected Mr. Shawn to read, and so when I first heard of my brother dying and immediately knew I would write about him, I thought of Mr. Shawn, but Mr. Shawn had just died, too, and I had seen Mr. Shawn when he was dead, and even then I wanted to tell him what it was like when he had died, and he would not have liked to hear that in any way, but I was used to telling him things I knew he didn't like, I couldn't help telling him everything whether he liked it or not. And so I wrote about the dead for the dead, and all along as I was writing I thought, When I am done with this I shall never write for Mr. Shawn again, this will be the end of anything I shall write for Mr. Shawn; but now I don't suppose that will be so. It was because I had neglected my brother when he was two years old and instead read a book that my mother gathered up all the books I owned and put them on a pile on her stone heap, sprinkling them with kerosene and then setting them alight; I cannot remember the titles of these books, I cannot remember what they were about (they would have been novels, at fifteen I read only novels), but it would not be so strange if I spent the rest of my life trying to bring those books back to my life by writing them again and again until they were perfect, unscathed by fire of any kind. For a very long time I had the perfect reader for what I would write and place in the unscathed books; the source of the books has not died, it only comes alive again and again in different forms and other segments. The perfect reader has died, but I cannot see any reason not to write for him anyway, for I can sooner get used to never hearing from him—the perfect reader—than to not being able to write for him at all.